POLICY STATEMENT

This book is not a rounded assessment of an already overblown subject; nor is it a direct reply to Lord Longford's inquiry as we don't know at the time of going to press what the exact result will be – although speculations have been made. *The ABZ of Pornography* is a pot-pourri of fact and quotation whose aim is to promote the acceptance of belief in freedom of expression. Our conclusions are no more radical than those reached by the American *Report of the Commission on Obscenity and Pornography*, by far the best research available.

Defending the rights of and, to some extent, the need for pornography can be less than elevating, especially when the material itself leaves much to be desired (in more senses than one). And where one personally fails to be 'turned on' by (say) accounts of rubber fetishism or close-ups of gaping vaginas, its effectiveness becomes hard to gauge. Frequently shoddy on its own terms, pornography can look grimly bizarre to the unaccustomed eye. Charges of exploitation, hypocrisy, degradation of women (and of men, incidentally) can easily be substantiated, while anti-pornography protest is a widespread phenomenon drawing support from the suburban grassroots rather than from a mere handful of crackpots.

But where the evidence of 'corruption' is so patently thin, the backlash potential of authoritarian censorship and the impertinent arrogance which judges 'on behalf of the less sophisticated' look infinitely worse than the pornography they seek to suppress.

John Kent's cartoons lend delightful support to our text.

The Editors, 1972

Edited by Richard Michael

With cartoons by John Kent

The ABZ of Pornography

Panther

Granada Publishing Limited
First published in 1972 by Panther Books Ltd
3 Upper James Street, London W1R 4BP

'Lord Longford' entry by David McKie
Additional material by David Adams

Made and printed in Great Britain by
Cox and Wyman Ltd, London, Reading and Fakenham
Set in Monotype Garamond

Australia – recommended price only

for William Miller

'The "positive" sense of the word "liberty" derives from the wish on the part of the individual to be his own master. I wish my life and decisions to depend on myself, not on external forces of whatever kind. I wish to be the instrument of my own, not of other men's, acts of will. I wish to be a subject, not an object; to be moved by reasons, by conscious purposes which are my own, not by causes which affect me, as it were, from the outside. I wish to be somebody, not nobody; a doer – deciding, not being decided for . . .'

Isaiah Berlin, *Two Concepts of Liberty*

SEX in ADVERTISING started, not with the nude, but with the motor car. A study by Dr Dichter, an American motivational researcher in the 1950s, explained the long-standing marketing puzzle of sedans *v.* convertibles (men were attracted to the showrooms by convertibles, but bought sedans) as a symbolic mistress *v.* wife struggle—men saw the convertible as a mistress but settled for the family sedan as a wife. And the sexual revolution in advertising—the increased use of nudes in the last three years—has had the same hard basis in research. Ad agencies don't throw in a nude just for good measure. As one ad executive put it: 'Ads don't make trends; it's too expensive to try to do so. They follow trends once they become apparent in the way people are acting generally ... Trends are the games of the few that become the serious pursuits of the many'—which we suppose is what happened with Adam and Eve.

The second thing about sexually explicit ads which most people don't realise is that many of them are designed to appeal, not to men, but to women. In the words of a leading ad agency, 'We're not trying to promote a sexual response, but a narcissistic response which is present in every woman. It's not sexual. It's not even sensual.' And the same statement exactly came from the man who made advertising respectable—Bob Wright, whose 1969 poster for Elliott's boots won a British Poster Design Award: 'We're trying to make something terribly feminine,' he said. And so say all of us!

We look first at the history of permissiveness in advertising; at the controllers of advertising standards and their attitudes; and lastly at the 'nude look' prevalent today.

BREAKING DOWN THE BARRIERS—LONDON

Well, they did. In 1968 to be precise, when Marilyn Rickard, for three years the leading lady of the Nelbarden swimsuit campaign, came to life and walked up an underground escalator in her bikini. Little did she know she was the last of a long line of pin-ups to push back the frontiers of London Transport's taste. Operating under a code which gives them freedom to refuse virtually any ad they like, the London Underground, reputedly the haven of the sexy ad, has always been more of a battleground on which the geography of permissiveness is repeatedly redefined. Nipples, for instance, are still out. London Transport has refused, among many, some posters that made headlines:

Vanessa Redgrave with her arms crossed over bare breasts advertising Ken Russell's **Isadora**;

in 1960 and 1970 posters for the Camden Arts Festival—arch-offenders—even though in 1970 the offending nude, Miss Carolee Schneeman, well-known for her nakedness in the cause of art, was standing in the middle of a group of fully-clothed artists, and the whole photo was enclosed in such a small circle that it was nearly invisible to the (naked) eye; also in 1970, a poster for Sue Davies' Photographers Gallery. The exhibition was entitled 'Four Masters of Erotic Photography' and this time LT objected to words, not pictures (the shot used was a harmless picture of a girl's face inside an apple). First, they refused Sue's slogan: 'This is the only picture they would let us use to advertise.' Then, they refused a reprinted poster simply because it contained the word 'Erotic'.

In the ding-dong battle between London Transport and the advertisers which, in the popular mythology of permissiveness, has become as famous as the battle between publishers and W. H. Smith and Sons, the advertisers have hit back by exploiting the very fact of LT censorship. Ring London Transport now and they will tell you rather sourly that, 'Of course, if you want some free publicity, it's always easy to print a poster you know we'll reject and then get the story in the papers.' And even on some posters they've accepted, advertisers have sometimes scored a point or two. A recent entirely innocuous ad for a horror movie *The Abominable Doctor Phibes* took up the 'teaser' patch over Phibes' face, stating 'We are not allowed to show this face. It's too horrible.'

BREAKING DOWN THE BARRIERS—OUT OF TOWN

If London Transport, and the Underground in particular, is the centre of the permissive *v.* reactionary struggle in London, out of town and nationally the field of combat is much wider. It's only three years since posters which simply featured girls in bikinis were running into trouble with local councils. In Lincoln, in 1968, a poster for National Savings of all things, was withdrawn by public library officials who commented: 'It might have been all right as a holiday poster, but it bears no relation to savings!' A beautiful example of the doublethink which attends some censorship: it's all right to be nude on the beach, but not when it's something to do with money. (National Savings spokesmen revealed that the poster had been a big success in mining areas.) Frinton and Walton Urban District Council rejected a poster for 'England's Friendliest Resort' (Frinton and Walton) which showed a rather dated drawing of a kid making sandcastles. He wasn't nude or anything, it's just that backsides aren't what friendliness is all about in Frinton and Walton. A similar classic was the storm over Exmouth's holiday poster showing a (fully clad except for shorts) model on a beach. Unfortunately, she was an American model on a Tunisian beach. 'It was a very controversial poster,' said a spokesman for the British Resorts Association, but he didn't say whether the complaints were because she was sexy or because she was foreign.

A more national row which made the headlines in most papers was over a BOAC poster which featured a gorgeous stewardess—her face and a few square inches of one bare shoulder—asking, 'Want to Get Off With Me?' Well, no, it doesn't win any prizes for the Original Slogan of the Year, but it hardly warranted the parliamentary indignation of, among others, Sir Cyril Black. The poster was withdrawn but the fashion for attacking BOAC and BEA continued. It was a favourite parliamentary sport in 1965. BOAC and BEA posters showing nothing more provocative than bikini-clad ladies on sun-drenched beaches were lambasted by MPs. One at least was replaced with a picture of a child clad in a straw hat on sun-drenched beaches, which is perverted if you like. Anyway, the whole furore was enough to make a private airline—BUA—voluntarily withdraw their 'own bikini girl Pauline Dukes' and substitute their 'one piece suit girl' (Pauline Dukes doubtless delighted at the double fee). Labour MP, James Dempsey (Coatbridge and Airdrie) said 'I am most certainly against any poster that shows scantily dressed women. I think posters of this kind are harmful and should not be allowed.' To date, no airline has reported any accidents involving planeloads of passengers whipped into erotic frenzy.

But the biggest national advertising rumpus was undoubtedly over

John Lennon and Yoko Ono's cover and posters for their 'Two Virgins' record. The cover, if you recall, showed them naked and hand in hand—from both sides. The posters concentrated on the back view. Many record stores refused to handle the album.

BILLPOSTING

It's not only national concerns and pop record companies that come unstuck. The same thing happened to the giant *Mirror* Group and their ill-fated *Mirror Colour Magazine*. They produced two posters advertising the first issue in 1969, and an article called, 'Do Clever Girls Miss Out On Sex?' The British Poster Association refused the bigger poster which was a side view of a nude in glasses. Perhaps the *Mirror Magazine* shouldn't have been too surprised. Billposting has always been one of the most old-fashioned areas of advertising, and even in anything-goes America a 70ft by 40ft nude in a yoga position with a flower in her mouth and an eye painted on her stomach (admittedly not your average nude) was banned from Broadway. It remained the Great White Way.

CODES OF HONOUR

The honour of advertisers is a ploy forever. London Transport's code mainly outlaws ads of a political or religious nature. It does, however, include a very wide justification for refusing almost anything.

Most modern ads *could* be said to 'depict or refer to indecency or obscenity' or be 'calculated to demoralise, extenuate crime, break the law or incite anyone to do so' or to 'foment social unrest' or 'contain illustrations or copy which are distorted or exaggerated in such a way as to convey false impressions'. More surprising are some specific bans—you cannot advertise contraceptives on the Underground and you mustn't plug any film refused permission for public exhibition. London Transport themselves admit that they accept ads today that they would never have accepted three or four years ago. Like any censor, they try to move with public taste, even if the result is never more than an uneasy liaison. Any advertiser can submit roughs and ideas to them for approval before going ahead with printing their ads. London Transport state that every major advertiser knows this and therefore they tend to regard 'banned' ads as some sort of plot by the advertisers to get Press publicity. London Transport's code covered £2,346,000 worth of advertising in 1970.

Television's standards are, as one might expect, both stricter and far more closely worded. They also ban advertising contraceptives plus, more unexpectedly, smoking cures, contact or corneal lenses, hair or scalp clinics, haemorrhoid treatments and products to treat alcoholism. In more general terms, the ITA's code states: 'The general principle which will govern all television advertising is that it should be legal, clean, honest and truthful.' (In other words, nothing like the programmes!) The only direct reference to sex comes, encouragingly enough, under the heading of 'Good Taste': 'No advertisement should offend against good taste or decency or be offensive to public feeling.' Ah, but who is to say how the public feel? And what happens if they're feeling sexy?

THE NUDE LOOK

One of the biggest distributors of sex books and magazines in Britain told us: 'The big breakthrough in the market has been in the last couple of years.' In an infinitely milder way, this applies to advertising also. Sex books have progressed from nudes to pubic hair and love positions – even the penis is beginning to peek through. Advertising has progressed to nudes, period, female and extremely tasteful. That's enough, however, to cause a rash of newspaper exposés, shrewdly decorated with reproductions of the ads that 'border on the pornographic', as *Reveille* describes them. 'The great nude boom,' said the *News of the World*, probing Annie Walker's agency – the main nude model agency. The models, it appeared, were all in favour and most of them seemed to have gone to great lengths to discuss their decision to appear starkers, with fathers, boyfriends etc., who were also all in favour. (The whole model industry is sickeningly domestic.) And the ads they were appearing in? Everything from El Cid sherry, perfumes (predictable) and after-shave ('Was It Him or His Piping Rock?' the lady wonders on the morning after) to, more originally, BRS Record Decks – a splendid shot of a couple in bed beside the record player, and the copy line: 'You're three beats out on the 27th bar of the third movement of Brahms' third symphony. And the phone rings.'

All good dirty fun, in fact. And tasteful in the extreme. The interesting thing about nude advertising is that it began and to date remains in the luxury, middle-class market – the world of cigars expensive drinks, fashion in all its aspects. And the ads which feature nudes are, for advertisements, restrained and intelligent, rarely explicit, making heavy use of puns and *double entente* which are far removed from any '3p. off this week' hard sell. Nude ads began, after all, in the glossy women's magazines. But their great leap forward was in March 1971 when Vivien Neves took it all off for Fisons in *The Times*. Apart from elevating Miss Neves almost immediately to Jean Shrimpton star-status, the ad was one of a series of eight which cost Fisons £11,560 and met with remarkably little reaction from the Top People who saw it. Most of them seemed to like it. But then it was in black and white. Ad director Mike Weston refused colour on the grounds that 'it might make the newspaper too much like *Playboy*', thus proving that admen move in realms of mysterious subtlety. The surprising thing about nudes is perhaps that they can still shock. When Gerry Andrews produced two live ones at the 1971 Motor Show, it was enough to get him a double-page spread in the *Sunday Mirror* – a publicist's dream. Admittedly, the girls were real live nudes, but they weren't appearing in public, only at a trade and Press review, and they were under strict instructions not 'to move their bodies while on show'. Their heads yes, but not the rest. Add to that the ruling that 'under no circumstances must the girls show their pubic hair ... a provocative display could have brought the house down'. Apart from sadly underestimating the erotic capacity of the average journalist, the Andrews stunt seems tame enough stuff: especially when you consider that the romance of the nude girl and the motor car has been going almost as long as the battle of the sexes proper. As far back as the 1930s, Simoniz was running ads with a nudist and a can of Simoniz. 'Don't let your car go nudist' was the caption.

CONCLUSION

In the last two or three years, the advertising industry has taken over the pin-up and made her respectable. As one artist is reported to have said of a top fashion magazine: 'Who needs pin-ups when you have this?' The industry has also, in line with the increasing sophistication of captions and copy on all subjects, become more frank, more witty and more subtle in its copy about sex (example: 'for the man contemplating his next casual affair' underneath a picture of a pair of suede shoes). But in this, as in everything, they have very much followed public taste rather than created it; and followed it at a considerable distance. What the industry has not done, and shows no sign of doing, is to imitate or use true sexually oriented material. Nude advertising began in women's magazines and the bulk of it is still directed at women, even when it advertises things like men's underwear (mostly bought by women *for* men). Hence the interesting point that a strand of the new advertising has been, not sexually oriented, but lesbian oriented. To quote David Bailey: 'Put a couple of butch-type girls together and the quality of the photograph doesn't matter. It's eye-stopping.' In an article in *The Observer*, critic Ronald Bryden came up with the following rationale for the nude look which is the best we've seen:

> In fact, physical modesty seems to have been a middle-class invention of the last century or so: A product of the first age in which a large proportion of the populace could afford a room for each member of the household, indoor plumbing and piped hot water. It is only in the modern middle-class home, with no servants, separate bathroom and bedrooms for each child, that the naked body has been able to become private to its owner.
>
> The coming of the flat and the bedsitter has intensified that privacy. But while they have made us strangers to one another's bodies, they have made us more familiar with our own. For the first time in modern cities, enormous numbers of adults live alone, with all the freedom and inhibition such privacy entails. The only other naked bodies they are likely to see are those of lovers, and models in magazine photographs; but their own can become known to them in a way impossible to members of a shared Victorian household, as they wander naked about their lonely, centrally-heated rooms, squeeze blackheads idly in front of mirrors or loiter in hot baths.
>
> This, obviously, is the audience at which the new nude publicity is directed. It is auto-erotic in implication, stressing the pleasures you can give your own body with the application of soaps and cosmetics, the touch of silk stockings and underwear. It is no

accident that female models are used to advertise women's products and male models men's. The intention is that you should identify the pictured body with your own, transfer the desirability of its superb proportions and suntanned flesh in your imagination to your own less glamorous physique.

The result has been a mental equation of nudity with sexuality. The only nakedness we know comes in a sexual context, in a form which leads us to blend our own bodies in fantasy with idealised shapes of impossible physical perfection.

That may be a pity or a good thing, but it is hardly pornographic or obscene.

ANIMALISM: Arguments against pornography are crucially linked to religious structures. The old, old struggle is seen as man's spiritual nature locked with his animal one. The Longford Committee is almost exclusively made up of declared Christians. Where such a valuable ethic seems to have got snarled up is in its assumption that the sex drive is, firstly, a threat to society, necessary for creation of the species, and only secondly (and that faintly) a source of great and continuous human pleasure. Controlled within marriage as a number one proviso, the alternative is ludicrously pictured as indiscriminate copulation in the streets. Clinging to the underbelly of this notorious pornographic monster are seen other grouped threats to society's sanctuary. And out of all this emerges Mr Identikit himself—a long-haired, unzipped youth who casts off his trousers with the same carelessness with which he votes for the Labour Party, rolling his joint and licking his chops as he beats teacher in the face with a placard marked Vietnam or Stormont, smashes car windows for anti-pollution purposes, derides the Queen, suffers from venereal disease, liberates the Negro and lives in a commune. Like most archetypes ...

ARTS COUNCIL REPORT (Conclusions):

1. It is not for the State to prohibit private citizens from choosing what they may or may not enjoy in literature or art unless there were incontrovertible evidence that the result would be injurious to society. There is no such evidence.
2. No crystal ball can tell us dogmatically whether more or less pornography would result from Repeal, but in any case there is a complete absence of evidence to suggest that sex in the arts, even when aphrodisiac in intention, has criminal or anti-social repercussions.
3. Though it is sometimes conjectured with no indisputable evidence that heavy and prolonged exposure to the portrayal of violence may not only reflect but also influence the standards of society, violence has been ubiquitous in the art, literature and Press of the civilised world for so long that censorship must by now be recognised as a totally inadequate weapon to combat it.

Indeed, laws available for the purpose including the Obscenity Acts are virtually never even invoked against it.

4. Since judges have to work in what is in effect a legal vacuum, the prosecution of an occasional book—usually the wrong one—often succeeds only in bringing the law into disrepute, without effectively preventing the distribution even of that book.

5. The very objective of the law is not even established, let alone identified, in concrete meaningful terms that could command acceptance. Although judges emphasise that an article cannot be condemned because it shocks or disgusts, in practice that is precisely what happens, since juries have no criterion to guide them.

6. It is impossible to devise a definition of obscenity that does not beg the question of a rational procedure for weighing depravity and corruption against artistic merit and 'the public good'.

7. When juries and defendants are without a comprehensible definition of the crime alleged, the defendant is left at the mercy of a personal opinion; which is a system of censorship rather than a system of law.

8. It is intolerable that a man should be criminally punished for an action that he has no means of ascertaining in advance is criminal.

9. Incitement to criminal behaviour is sufficiently covered by the ordinary law of incitement. To that extent the Obscenity Acts are redundant. In so far as they add the concept of a mere unintentional tendency toward crime as a punishable offence they are to be deplored.

10. It is an affront to both legal and common sense that incitement to a non-crime should be punishable as a crime; and worse when this doctrine is extended to a mere tendency.

11. No encouragement should be given to the concept of the State as 'custos morum' with its corollary that merely to shock is a criminal offence.

12. The proper sanction for breaches of taste or non-conformity with current mores should be social reprobation and not penal legislation.

THE BBC: The BBC is, according to many anti-pornographers, at the root of our moral pollution. In their literature, the Festival of Light condemns the BBC's permissiveness on pop records. ' "Wet Dream" reached the pop charts and has probably been piped into millions of homes,' they claim: in fact the BBC banned the record. And on sex education films:

> *Sexual Feeling* [one of the Learning about Life films for 14–16 year-olds] described in detail the practice of masturbation both for boys and girls. The speaker told the listening children that it was perfectly normal and even the most 'repressed people' were sexual privately ... *Falling in Love*: One gained the impression from the word chosen for the man and woman—'partners'—and the direct immediate link with contraception, that this programme was not intended to describe the married state ...

A Burnley schoolmaster, Robert Clegg, has also endeared himself to the anti-BBC lobby with a speech about sex education:

> A few weeks ago, at the time when the previews of the sex programmes were being broadcast, we had on the same evening a 'Panorama' programme dealing with sex education, and also a 'Horizon' programme which concerned itself with the new science of 'sexology'. Amongst the so-called experts appearing on the 'Horizon' programme were two from America, William Masters and Virginia Johnson, who are the joint authors of a best-selling book called *Human Sexual Response*. I know nothing about the book, apart from a description by Mr Masters which I have read of a perfectly incredible mechanical device with which, for the purpose of his researches, some of his female subjects actually had sexual relations.
>
> Besides writing books, Mr Masters, I understand, is very much concerned with sex education in America ... And it is rather striking that he and his associate should come over here, presumably at the invitation of the BBC, to peddle their disgusting wares on British television, just when the BBC is setting up its own programme on sex education ... All of which seems to me to add up to some kind of campaign by the BBC in favour of what we've got into the habit of calling 'permissiveness' and of which sex education is very much a part. Whoever they are, they [the authors of the sex education programmes] are doing something

which has been regarded for countless generations as one of the most revolting of crimes. They are setting out, with their benevolent voices, their parental manner, their beautiful arty pictures, even with musical accompaniment, to destroy the innocence of a whole generation of young children.

BESTIALITY: Analism includes all sorts of activity centred on the rectum. These start with buggery (or sodomy, which in certain legal definitions can also include fellatio and bestiality), and go through 'anal kisses' and rectal stimulation (the anus is an erogenous zone) to the fairly common buttock-fetishism. The pornography surrounding anal fixations similarly varies from soft-core photographs of fleshy bottoms to detailed descriptions of buggery. Freud made the anal phase one of the stages of his libido theory; certain traits, such as miserliness, are attributed to a fixation at this stage. Analism is also linked to coprophilia and sadism. Bestiality is sexual activity with animals and is very much to the fore in Scandinavian pornography: one pornographer is supposed to keep an animal farm specifically for certain publications—a case more for the RSPCA than for Lord Longford, perhaps. As an actual activity, Kinsey found, one male in twelve seems to have used an animal for sexual gratification at some time; three to four per cent of women interviewed had indulged in animal sex play, most of these with domestic pets. With man-animal sex, much was in country districts. The pornography of bestiality (also known as zoöphilia or zoörasty) shows coitus between animals and women, which is in reality very rare, and most infrequently masturbation of animals by men, which in fact is the most common. Coitus with men features in about the same proportion as real-life statistics suggest, though in circumstances (men and women in group sex with animals) that are totally at variance with any known activity. Favourite animals are those with large sexual organs, notably horses and mules, and those with bizarre genitalia, such as hogs (who have, as a matter of interest, corkscrew-shaped penises). Presumably the attraction is in the size of the animal's penis (usually shown being sucked by a girl), since actual sexual response to animals as sexual partners is rare. As a ritual, bestiality is to be found in many religions and it occurs in various forms of mythology and, apparently, in certain black magic rites.

BILLY GRAHAM: has expressed his fundamentalist approach to pornography in addition to a vigorous disguise whilst researching the amazing sights of America's 42nd Street. *Time* magazine printed the result (July 1969):

Graham:

> One day I put on dark glasses and a hat and pasted on long sideburns, and I went to some of these stores in New York. I had thought that Sweden was bad, but Sweden hasn't gone near to the depths of various sex deviations and obsessions that we have gone. I suppose there are sections of this country that have sunk as low as anything in history, because in the days of Sodom and Gomorrah and Pompeii and Rome they didn't have the presses or the motion pictures to stimulate all of this ...
>
> God never meant that people were to wear clothes. He meant we were to be nude. But we were in a state of innocence. Then sin came into the human race and became a blood poisoning. The first thing that Adam and Eve did after their rebellion against God was to see themselves naked, and they were ashamed and they sewed fig leaves and clothed themselves ... Certainly a woman should never disguise the fact that she is a woman. A woman's body is very beautiful. But this emphasis on nudity, which stimulates sensuality—this is what is going to destroy society. It's interesting to me that in the Soviet Union, Cuba and China, they're trying to build a strong society that they hope will ultimately conquer the world. But they don't allow this kind of sexuality ...
>
> When I was 17, 18, 19, 20, I was interested in sex—and if I had all of this thrown at me at that time, I don't know whether or not I could have withstood it ...
>
> The Bible says that the reason the flood came was that lawlessness had spread all over the world and sensuality had spread all over the world. Jesus said, 'As it was in the days of Noah, so shall it be when the Son of Man comes back.' He said there would be a world wide rebellion. Well, we see that going on now. He

said that there would be an obsession with sex at the end of history, and we see all of that going on.

BOOKS: Pornographic books are dealing with the most effective form of fantasy stimulus. Written 'hot bits', 'thumbed bits', 'rude bits' excite the average recipient even more than close-up cinema. Human imagination ...

Nevertheless, excluding a few world best-sellers which have high sexual content, although not necessarily pornographic (at least under the old law of overall intent) the book has technically been demoted in the pornographic league, for the 'dirty bookshop' down the libelled Charing Cross Road is more likely to be crowded with sex *magazines* and 8mm stag movies, where that old stand-by from the saucy stalls of Paris has finally died, suffocated in its cellophane wrapper. For with the wraps off, the escalation of eroticism diminishes beyond recall down to our own adolescence when Alberto Moravia's *Women of Rome* was whispered about excitedly in corners.

Books in the dock (including the one responsible for Prosecution Counsel Mr Griffith-Jones's immortal question: 'Is it a book that you would even wish your wife or your servants to read?') will be dealt with under *Trials* because here we are examining patterns, and our main situation as a mini America. The USA's 'Obscenity' commission pretty well mirrors the British position although America is still in 'advance' of us with her open sales, notably of sexual print at news-stands.

'Self-labelled "adults only" printed materials are of far less economic importance than are mass market publications,' says the commission. For example, the combined copy sales of all 'adults only' magazines in a year are less than one month's sales of *Reader's Digest*. Separate 'secondary' channels of national and local wholesale distribution and local retail sales, have been created for this 'adults only' market. However, there is an overlap of sexually orientated materials between the mass and the 'adult' market; some publishers produce material for both, and many other publishers constantly seek to expand distribution of their 'secondary' products into the mass market ...

SEX PULP BOOKS UNTIL THE LATE 1960s

The sexual content of paperback books published for the 'adults only' market has become progressively 'stronger' in the past decade, primarily because of court decisions involving books such as *Tropic of Cancer* and *Fanny Hill*.

Until the mid-1960s, most paperback books published for the secondary market were known as 'sex pulps'. These followed a rather rigid set of ground rules – vulgar terms describing sexual acts, genitalia, excretion, etc., were not used, but euphemistic or symbolic language was substituted; the books consisted of a series of sexual adventures tied together by a minimal plot; sexual foreplay was described in great detail, but the mechanics of the sex act was not; and much of the sexual content was left to the imagination of the reader.

By the late 1960s, however, the 'sex pulp' formula had become relatively passé. A new breed of sexually orientated secondary books came on to the market, in which all restraints upon both language and descriptions of sexual activity were eliminated. In many, there was little pretence of a story line; many books were little more than a compilation of non-stop sexual activity.

Some paperback novels of the 'sex pulp' type of the early 1960s are still published, probably because a portion of the market prefers less explicit material. However, the industry's criterion for 'sex pulp' books has been broadened; this classification now includes any paperback which is badly written, edited and typeset, and is apparently aimed at relatively poorly educated readers, irrespective of the degree of explicitness of its language or descriptions of sexual activity.

WHOLLY TEXTUAL SEX-ORIENTATED PAPERBACK BOOKS IN THE SECONDARY MARKET 1969–1970

Virtually every English language book thought to be obscene when published, and many similar books translated into English, have been reissued by secondary publishers. The entire stockpile of 'classic erotic literature' (e.g. *The Kama Sutra,* Frank Harris, De Sade, etc.) published over centuries has thus come on to the market. Another type of sexually orientated book (see *Sex Education*) has become popular in the last few years—pseudo-medical, alleged case-history of sexual activity. Although such books purport to be written by medical doctors or PhDs, they primarily consist of graphic descriptions of sexual activity.

As of 1970, publishers of sex-orientated, wholly textual paperback books are convinced that there are no legal restrictions on the content of any wholly textual publication. As a result, 'adults only' paperback books published and sold in the United States cannot possibly be exceeded in candour, graphic description of sexual activity or use of explicit language. The overwhelming majority of these books are intended for a heterosexual male readership. Almost no such books are written for a female market. Perhaps 10 per cent or more are directed at the male homosexual market, and less than 5 per cent are specifically written for any of the various fetishes.

ILLUSTRATED PAPERBACK BOOKS, 1969–1970

In the past two or three years, some publishers have included photographs in their books. Initially, such paperbacks included photographs in which young females posed with the focus of the camera directly upon their genitalia. In 1968 and 1969, however, two additional types came into the market which revolutionised the sexual content of illustrated paperback books. One was the illustrated 'marriage manual' containing photographs of couples engaging in sexual intercourse, 'for an educational purpose'. The most recent marriage manuals of this type depict fellatio and cunnilingus in addition to vaginal intercourse (penetration shown in detail). The second 'breakthrough' occurred in 1969 with the publication of books purporting to be serious studies of censorship and pornography. These books contain illustrations ranging from Oriental and European erotic art to reproductions of 'hard-core' photographs taken from Danish magazines which graphically depict sex activities such as vaginal and anal penetration, fellatio and cunnilingus. Following this lead, a number of publications containing 'hard-core' photographs with textual commentary have been published and are in circulation in many major metropolitan areas.

To some extent, therefore, the pictorial content of a number of paperbacks published and sold in the United States has reached the level of sexual explicitness found in Danish material. However,

Danish-type 'pornographic' magazines, consisting entirely of photographs of sexual activity, have yet to be sold openly in this country; domestic publishers apparently believe that the inclusion of text is required to provide a legal defence in the event of an obscenity prosecution (The Report of the US Commission on Obscenity and Pornography).

It is perhaps worth pointing out that British rules still censor genitalia and above all the erect penis (see *Sex Education*).

Britain, of course, like many other countries, has a very active mail order service for books which are frequently advertised in men's magazines. They share, in addition to a few hilarious titles, that other common denominator among all 'blurbs', unabating enthusiasm for the product.

We just have space for a few such titles and better still their hyperbolic 'come-ons'.

> *White Thighs*—inside secrets of the Nymphomaniac. Crammed full of lascivious sex orgies, of women who build their lives on their bodies and the thrills it gives men. One man is never enough. EXCITING, UNINHIBITED READING. ILLUSTRATED.
>
> *Miss Butch—The Shocking Candid Facts* of the secret desires and sex ways of a Lesbian. Her wants and her needs were unanswered by a man—By any man—and she tried them all! The secret desires, searches, seductions and sexways that form the Lesbian Way are all explicitly revealed in this absorbing book. FULLY ILLUSTRATED.
>
> *The 69 Pleasures of Love.* This book has EVERYTHING for the Adult reader—translated from the French *Soixante Neuf*, it covers every aspect of the sex act with most vivid photos and illustrations throughout. Every person who has read 'Love Positions' must buy this one—Obviously the PLEASURES are a natural follow-up to the POSITIONS! We cannot recommend this book too highly.
>
> *Hot Pants.* Literally I feel 'hot' in my panties whenever I feel there is a chance of sex with a boy. This 'heat' rises from my genitals and courses throughout the whole of my body, giving me almost instant nipple erection and certainly making my clitoris feel terribly sensitive. I then become violently aware of my panties and what they are covering and I want them torn off by this fellow.

> *Maid For Pleasure.* These unabashed accounts will shock and amaze you. Held in the Satanic power of a lustful debaucher, she revealed her insatiable sex needs. Read about the bizarre demands made on her, and the degradation she went through ... and how this lust-filled beauty took the unusual in her stride. ILLUSTRATED.

This is the mixture as it has always been, now surfaced from below the counter, breathless alliteration and earnest appeal to shock-value taboo-breaking, with standard references to the 'adult' mind of the purchaser who must cherish his 'specialist interest' as 'a collector of erotica'.

Beyond this middle point, and we have largely quoted from middle-of-the-road mail order brochures, lies the question of high class pornography or pornography as art. Susan Sontag in a thoughtful, incomprehensible essay refers to De Sade's *120 Days of Sodom* as

> probably the most ambitious pornographic book ever conceived (in terms of scale), a kind of summa of the pornographic imagination; stunningly impressive and upsetting, even in the truncated form, part narrative and part scenario, in which it has survived.

Eliot Fremont-Smith said of the *Story of O*:

> The test is severe-sexual in method, psychological in substance ... the artistic interest here has precisely to do with the use not only of erotic materials but also erotic methods, the deliberate stimulation of the reader as a part of and means to a total, authentic literary experience.

Which makes a point even if it sounds like 'Pseuds' Corner'.

In case we get carried away by all this engaging intellectualism, we attach ourselves limpet-like to a noble statement by John Mortimer, Q.C.

> I would like to form a society for the Defence of Bad Literature. Every writer has, it seems to me, the inalienable right to fail, and I think it's highly inequitable that the talented should be permitted access to erotic fields denied to the clumsy, talentless majority. We should not only be able to defend to the death other people's right to say things with which we disagree; we must allow them to say it in abominable prose.

CENSORSHIP: 'The main discussion about censorship, however, centres on sex, excretion and violently inflicted pain. It is all about the body and the primitive extremes of pain and pleasure. We are embarrassed to show these in public. And particularly to a public whose individual members are unknown to each other. The famous device of the club performance illustrates this last point nicely. It is nothing more than a legal wangle now, but it rests on a very substantial superstition – that people bound together by some formal affinity (and therefore theoretically, at least, known to each other) are somehow protected from the black magic of collectively experienced depravity.

This is one of the reasons why TV censorship is so much stricter when it comes to questions of sex and violence. Quite apart from the fact that telly creeps like a cat burglar into the sleeping household, there is the question of the vast, fragmented, mutual anonymity of the audience.

It is easy to see how this ban on carnal spectacle came into existence. One of the things that gives it away is the list of bodily functions, pains and pleasures the imitations of which are NOT banned on the stage. Gluttony never runs into any trouble. No one ever shuts down a pie-eating contest and the film censor never touched the disgusting scenes in *Henry the Eighth* where Charles Laughton gobbled a chicken as a whole. Sloth is all right and so is anger. Even fear unto death is no problem; except for children, of course. The censor is only moved to act when it comes to the display and exercise of what we call the private parts.

Censorship here is nothing more than a legal corollary of public modesty. It is part and parcel of the whole delicate machinery of etiquette to whose changes its own development is tied. So long as we continue to lock ourselves in segregated lavatories, fasten our flies and sit with our knees together when travelling on buses, the abolition of formal censorship will change very little in the content of public performance.' (Jonathan Miller, *The Guardian* inquiry into the Permissive Society.)

THE CHURCH and pornography are inseparable. The existence of pornography and its suspected ability to deprave and morally corrupt all who sample it (willingly or unwillingly: the anti-pornographers believe that it is thrust at us) has given Christianity a new sense of purpose and Christian evangelists a new lease of life.

Lord Longford, Cliff Richard, Malcolm Muggeridge, Mary Whitehouse and the organisers of the Festival of Light have something in common. They are all ardent campaigners against pornography, yes. But, more of a coincidence, they are all devout practising Christians. They all attack pornography because they see sex as God-given and any interference by mortals in the doling out of erotic experiences as simply anti-Christian. The anti-pornography movement is not simply a moral one, or one spontaneous reaction by an average cross-section of the general public against something they find aesthetically, politically, ethically or culturally objectionable. It is a specifically Christian campaign against a phenomenon that contradicts the Christian ethic, and so the organisation of protest has taken on a Christian sense of mission. In other words, for the average man, who is really not a devout Christian of any denomination (and the campaigners are noticeably Catholic and evangelical), the real issues of pornography are in danger of being glossed over or incidental to the specifically Christian moral objections.

Sex must be confined to marriage—and even here only for the purpose of procreation, says the devout Catholic; certainly *within* marriage, says the traditional churchman and at the very least within a meaningful emotional relationship, say the more progressive 'New Theologians' (whom we shall come to shortly). For any Pauline Christian, sex as a pure pleasure is anathema. And pornography, whatever we take it to mean, at root is about sex without any ramifications outside corporeal lust.

Kinsey found that 'devoutly religious backgrounds had prevented some of the females and males [from the 1,240 who participated in his two studies] from ever engaging in certain types of sexual activity'. His statistics reveal that pre-marital coitus, extra-marital coitus and homosexual activity showed a marked correlation with the subjects' religious devotion, and that even frequent marital coitus was frowned upon by some religious males. And although the degree of religious devotion continued to affect those males who finally did become involved in the morally disapproved types of activity, with women the involvement didn't seem to depend at all on the degree of religious devotion. Since it's generally up to the man to initiate—and certainly to complete—coitus, and Kinsey revealed that the very religious men tend to keep the coital rate low because of their religious beliefs, there must be some frustrated wives, as well as mistresses, who are quite capable of relinquishing their religious prejudices against sex but whose husbands and lovers won't. Further, Kinsey found that 21 per cent of his devoutly Catholic females had not reached orgasm by the age of 35 even though most of them were married and indulging in regular intercourse; this compares with 2 per cent of the non-practising Catholics.

Kinsey's results reflect from the teachings of, not so much Christ, as of the Church fathers—notably Saints Paul and Augustine, both converts and all the more rabid and moralistic for it. Saint Paul, for example, laid the foundations of the Christian attitude to sex when he wrote:

> In fact, this seems to be the rule, that every single time I want to do good it is something evil that comes to hand. In my inmost self I dearly love God's law (or reason's law), but I can see that my body follows a different law that battles against the law which my reason dictates. This is what makes me a prisoner of that law of sin which lives inside my body.

Paul emphasised too the traditional Judeo-Christian abhorrence of homosexuality:

> God has abandoned [the pagans] to degrading passions; their women have turned from natural intercourse to unnatural practices and their menfolk have given up natural intercourse to be consumed by passion for each other, men doing shameless things with men and getting an appropriate reward for their perversion.

Progressive Christians today are still trying to inculcate a more tolerant approach. The Society of Friends, whose *Towards a Quaker View of Sex* remains one of the most farsighted and humanitarian documents of Christian theology, said:

> Surely it is the nature and quality of a relationship that matters. One must not judge it by its outward appearance, but by its inner worth. Homosexual affection can be as selfless as hetero-

sexual affection, and therefore we cannot see that it is in some way morally worse.

The Quakers were roundly condemned by many traditional Christians.

Traditional Christianity has always maintained that any sexual activity outside marriage is evil, whether the sex be homosexual, pre- or extra-marital, oral or whatever. Any celebration of sexuality, whether in the form of erotic sculpture or elementary pornography, would be condemned by the strict traditional Christian. Alex Comfort, one of the traditional Christian's main targets, pointed out in his *Sex and Society*:

> In dealing with Christianity as an influence, we are not dealing with the teaching or beliefs of its most intelligent or most liberal exponents, and modern Christian ethical writers who point to the exaggeration of Christian anti-sexuality in psychological literature must face the reply that it is with the consequences on the public attitude towards sexual conduct, rather than on the intention of the teachers, that our estimate of Christianity must rest. Whatever Christianity may have contributed to the growth of our culture in other fields, it seems undeniable that in sexual morals and practice its influence has been less healthy than that of other world religions ... it created a system of sexual ethics and an attitude towards sexuality, at once rigid, antagonistic to the observed facts of human character and behaviour, and based upon fear, to which the imminent end of the world added point.

But traditional Christian views of chastity have, in recent years, been undermined within the Churches themselves. Over 20 years ago, in 1951, Pope Pius XII affirmed that it was right that 'husband and wife shall find pleasure and happiness of mind and body'. Protestants went further and approved contraception, thus refuting the traditional Pauline-Augustinian insistence on sex-for-procreation-only and thus opened a 'gate to a new depth and joy in personal relationships between husband and wife', as the Lambeth bishops claimed in 1958.

At the same time, progressive Churchmen were rethinking traditional Christian morals; in Britain they were signalled by publications like *Towards a Quaker View of Sex* (1963), *Soundings* (1962) and *Objections to Christian Belief* (1963) both edited by the

Rev. A. R. Vidler, *Honest to God* (1963) by John Robinson, Bishop of Woolwich, and *No New Morality* (1964) by Douglas Rhymes, Canon of Southwark Cathedral. In fact there were two schools, the Cambridge Divinity dons and the South Bank clerics, while in the middle came the traditional reaction in *The New Morality* (1964) by Sir Arnold Lunn and Garth Lean. The advocates of the 'New Morality' (a title they rejected) took a humanitarian attitude to sexual relations. The Quakers wrote:

> We shall have reason to say that sexuality, looked at dispassionately, is neither good nor evil—it is a fact of nature ... It seemed to us that morals, like the Sabbath, were made for man, not man for morals, and that, as society changes and modes of conduct with it, we must always be searching below the surface of human behaviour—to discover what is in fact happening to people, what they are seeking to express, what motives and intentions that are satisfying, what fruits, good or bad, they are harvesting.

Dr Robinson stated:

> One cannot start from the position 'sex relations before marriage' or 'divorce' are wrong or sinful in themselves ... the only intrinsic evil is lack of love.

Harry Williams, a contributor to both Cambridge books, thought:

> a great deal of what Christians often call virtue on closer inspection turns out to be cowardice.

On the Continent the idea of 'situation ethics' or 'contextual ethics' was put forward principally by Dietrich Bonhoeffer (whose *Ethics* appeared in 1955), who justified his complicity in the plot to kill Hitler with the assertion that 'principles are only tools in the hand of God, soon to be thrown away as unserviceable'. The American 'situationalist' Joseph Fletcher believes that 'the freedom to make responsible decisions' is more important than obedience to 'prefabricated rules of conscience' and that

> even a transient sex liaison, if it has the elements of caring, of tenderness and selfless concern, is better than a mechanical, egocentric exercise of 'conjugal rights' between two uncaring or antagonistic marriage partners.

CINEMA: What can one say about the dear old movies except that thousands of cinemas round the globe have closed since the 1950s advent of television, that Hollywood as a Mecca collapsed in the middle 1960s, that films *on* television, and sexploitations, are meant to keep the industry alive? It is the strongest medium for visual sex—poetry or porn—and like other subjects in this A–Z, there is increasing indistinction between its general legitimate market (i.e. films for wide circuit release) and its specialised club–stage–blue picture market, which in the past anyway has profited from shock value. Also, like other subjects here, it has a large secondary market in the shape this time of sexy film stills (see *G String*).

A late taboo to be wrangled over was the much-publicised question of allowing female pubic hair. This was finally decided as yes in 1969, for the ordinary British viewer, but local Watch Committees can still come up with a few surprises. The next taboo to be lifted almost immediately, though not in the anatomical sense, meant fleeting glimpses of the penis, and Ken Russell's sequence of Oliver Reed and Alan Bates sporting in the nude was hailed as the breakthrough (a perfectly tasteful wrestling episode which quite failed to capture the meaning from the book). Simulated intercourse (at least in head and shoulders close-ups or with bizarre stipulations like the horizontal bed lover keeping one foot on the floor) has been a feature of the movies for most of its history, despite the rigours of the Hollywood Protection Code and its stern admonitions against 'open-mouthed' kissing. Actual intercourse with genitals in action is a last dividing line between pornography and official tolerance, yet even here a more respectable output has grown under the guise of sex instruction films (see *Sex Education*).

It isn't true to say that the old blue film 'aint what she used to be', because the same rough-cut tat is still touted on metropolitan street corners—not just in London and Soho either. But well-defined pornographic films need all the group gropes they can invent to stave off rival eroticism at the local.

Past cinema codes are not only fun in retrospect, where at the time they pushed the exasperated film maker's sense of the 'ridiculous' to the limit; they show how social values need to change and how the flesh is continually confused with the devil. In other words, yet again, sex and nakedness have got all muddled up with religious restrictions and never more so than in the case of the Hollywood Production Code, drafted in 1929 by two midwestern Roman Catholics, and fiercely shadowed by the Catholic Legion of Decency, founded in 1934, a thorn in Hollywood's side for over thirty years until alterations were made in the mid-1960s. As Philip French points out in his excellent book, *The Movie Moguls*:

> During this period, the Legion handed out moral classifications ranging from A–1, which meant 'Morally Unobjectionable for General Patronage', to Class C for 'Condemned', and circulated its decisions among Catholic communities throughout the world.
>
> To appease the Church, it was therefore necessary to make the Production Code mandatory and impose sanctions on its breach. Accordingly in 1934, the ex-journalist Joseph I. Breen, an Irish-American Catholic of Hay's Hollywood branch, was put in charge of the Studio Relations Department which was re-named the Production Code Administration, with power to withhold a certificate and Seal of Approval. A fine of 25,000 dollars was established for any member company releasing a film without a Seal.

The occasion hardly arose since all the large cinemas were members of the Motion Picture Producers and Distributors Assn. of America Inc.

THE AMERICAN MOTION PICTURE PRODUCTION CODE OF 1930–SOME EXTRACTS:

Mankind has always recognised the importance of entertainment and its value in rebuilding the bodies and souls of human beings. But it has always recognised that entertainment can be of a character harmful to the human race, and in consequence, has clearly distinguished between: Entertainment which tends to improve the race or at least to recreate and rebuild human beings exhausted with the realities of life; and Entertainment which tends to deprave human beings or to lower their standard of life and living.

GENERAL PRINCIPLES regarding plots dealing with sex, passion, and incidents relating to them: All legislators have recognised clearly that there are in normal human beings emotions which react naturally and spontaneously to the presentation of certain definite manifestations of sex and passion:

(*a*) The presentation of scenes, episodes, plots etc. which are deliberately meant to excite these manifestations on the part of the audience is always wrong, is subversive to the interest of society and a peril to the human race.

(*b*) Sex and passion exist and consequently must sometimes enter into the stories which deal with human beings:

1. Pure love, the love of a man for a woman permitted by the law of God and man, is the rightful subject of plots. The passion arising from this love is not the subject for plots.

2. Impure love, the love of man and woman forbidden by human and divine law, must be presented in such a way that (*a*) it is clearly known by the audience to be wrong, (*b*) its representation does not exist to incite sexual reaction, mental or physical, in an ordinary audience, (*c*) it is not treated as matter for comedy.

VULGARITY: may be carefully distinguished from obscenity. Vulgarity is the treatment of low, disgusting, unpleasant subjects which decent society considers outlawed from normal conversation.

OBSCENITY: is concerned with immorality, but has the additional connotation of being common, vulgar and coarse.

COSTUMES. GENERAL PRINCIPLES:

1. The effect of nudity or semi-nudity upon the normal man or woman, and much more upon the young person, has been honestly recognised by all lawmakers and moralists.

2. Hence the fact that the nude or semi-nude body may be beautiful does not make its use in the films moral. For in addition to its beauty, the effects of the nude or semi-nude body on the normal individual must be taken into consideration.

3. Nudity or semi-nudity used simply to put 'punch' into a picture comes under the heading of immoral actions as treated above. It is immoral in its effect upon the average audience.

4. Nudity or semi-nudity is sometimes apparently necessary for the plot. Nudity is never permitted.

Particular Principles:

1. The more intimate parts of the human body are the male and female organs and the breasts of a woman:

(*a*) They should never be uncovered.

(*b*) They should not be covered with transparent or translucent material.

(*c*) They should not be clearly and unmistakably outlined by the garment.

BEDROOMS: Their use in a comedy or farce (on the principle of the so called 'bedroom farce') is wrong, because they suggest sex laxity and obscenity.

RELIGION: Ministers of religion in their characters of ministers should not be used in comedy, as villains, or as unpleasant persons. (Note: The reason for this is not that there are not such ministers of religion but because the attitude towards them tends to be an attitude towards religion in general.)

The 1956 code still fretted over 'lustful and open-mouth kissing'.

The British Board of Film Censors was set up in July 1912.

First President, George Redford, aiming to keep the cinema 'clean and free of any stigma, even of vulgarity'.

Topics to be banned:

No cremations.

No final, tear-impelling scenes at funerals.

No scenes representing murder, sudden death, or suicide.

No mixed bathing.

No 'compromising situations'.

No cock fights, no dog fights, and nothing where unnecessary cruelty is brought in, either to man or beast.

All Biblical scenes to be watched very carefully.

No Sovereigns, Judges, Ministers or such high officials of the land to be treated in an unbecoming or undignified or ridiculous manner, and no living individual was to be lampooned.

As quoted by Richard Findlater, from *The History of British Film* Vol. 1. Rachael Low (Allen and Unwin 1948).

Britain's growing cinematic freedoms were charted by the now retired film censor, John Trevelyan, talking to Weston Taylor, in a 1968 article for the *News of the World.*

(1) Jane Russell in *The Outlaw* (December 1946) ('Hollywood's projection of voluptuous womanhood').

(2) Jamie O'Hara in *Garden of Eden* (January 1957) ('It was the first of the nudist pictures, and we didn't know what the public reaction would be. We sent the film round to the local authorities. They didn't object, and there was considerable public acceptance of this picture, which opened the screens to nudity').

(3) Laurence Harvey in *Room at the Top* (January 1959) ('Very frank love scenes but there was nothing I objected to because it was one of the first British films which was concerned with real, recognisable people and their emotional problems').

(4) Albert Finney in *Saturday Night and Sunday Morning* (October 1960) (more realism).

(5) Luis Bunuel's *Viridiana* (May 1962) ('a great artist with something special to say'). It was condemned as blasphemous by the Vatican and General Franco ordered the film negative to be burned.

(6) Ingmar Bergman's *The Silence* (April 1964). ('Because of Bergman's integrity we passed certain scenes, including one concerning masturbation.')

(7) Agnes Varda's *Le Bonheur* (July 1965). ('There were lengthy shots of bare breasts but we regarded this as a tender film about love rather than sex ... Mind you we tend to be rather more generous with foreign language films. The dialogue cannot be followed as closely as in the routine pictures.')

(8) Michael Caine in *Alfie* (March 1966). ('He "laid" all the birds, didn't he? But what was important was why Alfie did it and what happened to him in the long run.')

(9) Carol White in *Poor Cow* (December 1967). ('There was nothing wrong or unusual in seeing Carol White's nipples in the photographic studio sequence in *Poor Cow*. There has been more shown of actresses in other films. But this (and No. 10) marked the first time we admitted certain words and expressions such as "silly bugger". We did so because such phrases and dialogue belong to the kind of characters who were being portrayed.')

(10) Suzy Kendall in *Up The Junction* (January 1968). Since then of course, the floodgates, as they say ...

THE SUB PORNO MARKET AND TRUE BLUE MOVIES: Eves without leaves having fun in the sun expanded by the mid-sixties into more active moments beyond the natural call of volleyball. A Nudie maker called Erskie Fife summed it up as follows:

> Nudies are not – repeat not – pornography ... Look – what does your average moviegoer go to see? I'll tell you – sex, violence, nudity and, hopefully, a healthy dollop of perversion thrown in. You've only got to look at the commercial films that really make money to know I'm right. Okay, the Nudie format is to deliver the goods without confusing and boring the viewer with things like involved love stories and plots ... Regular Hollywood movies are like sandwiches with mostly bread but a first-class nudie is all meat – in more ways than one.

Meat then, or what old-fashioned printers poetically call 'hot meat hanging out', is mostly what it's about. In Britain, audience expectation (other than bona fide sensation stirrers like the frank language in Joyce's *Ulysses*) finds a legalised outlet in the club cinema. One of the more engaging accounts of club activities came from Alban Blawn for *Time-Out*.

> And now the completely static talking idiot show, as recorded dead at the House of Lords, April 21st, 1971. First, the star of our show, The Earl of Longford: 'I hold in my hand (in his hand, ladies and gentlemen!) a piece of hard pornography which a headmistress recently found in the possession of a girl of 14.'

The films listed in *Time Out*'s Cinema Voyeur column have great curiosity value. This is enhanced by the almost total lack of information available on their content; even the publicity is minimal, consisting usually of a simple announcement in the *Evening Standard* heralding the appearance of another sizzler with some name like *Ramrodder* or *Hard Man Good to Find*.

It is curiosity which makes the sex cinema club circuit the goldmine that it is. The clubs are run on the oldest fairground barkers' hustle: promise them everything, give them what you can get away with and stay legal. If censorship were to be abolished they would disappear in their present form overnight, for their one unvarying sales pitch is that the films are uncensored, and therefore promise more sexual explicitness than that permitted by the Board of Film

Censors. This is true only in that the films are not checked by the censors, but they are still frequently cut as, without a certificate, the promoters risk prosecution by the police.

The Earl of Longford (Lab.) said that the most objectionable films were those shown in so-called clubs, which were free to make the worst possible use of the best of all possible worlds.

The first sex film club was the Compton in Old Compton Street, which opened in 1961, run by the former managers of a striptease club and a local cinema, Messrs. Klinger and Tenser. The first films were what is known in the trade as 'nudie-cuties', i.e. virtually plotless epics using nudist camps as locations and featuring the occasional bouncing breast. The hero and heroine ended up holding hands and the sun set on yet another game of volleyball. Despite the extraordinary success of these films, Compton was in serious financial straits by the mid-sixties, due primarily to an over-ambitious production programme. Tenser and Klinger left, and the company was taken over by a big shareholder, Leslie Elliot, who had also dabbled in film production. The name was changed to Cinecenta, and after much turmoil the new set-up was also dedicated to a policy of sex films. They were the only ones that consistently made money. In 1969 the Classic chain began converting some of its less profitable cinemas into clubs, and now has a chain of sixteen part-time and eight full-time Tatler cinema clubs not including the London ones, while Cinecenta has eleven (including the four in London). The majority of the films shown at these clubs are imported by Cinecenta.

Lord Nugent of Guildford (C.) said older people mostly protected themselves against a continuous flow of pornographic material by ignoring it. But young people found it difficult to resist.

The average club is small, or intimate, depending on your point of view. The audience is made up exclusively of males, usually alone. No one ever laughs, and most of the films are watched in dead silence; though one gathers that members are quick to complain at injudicious cuts. They keep coming back for more: it is possible to go into a club at 12 a.m. on a Monday morning and find it half full. And the films are terrible.

The Earl of Longford said that some of the films shown to the public were bad enough but the ones in clubs were understood to be a good deal worse.

The great majority are American. A large part of the industry is now geared to producing these sexploitation movies, movies which are quick and easy to make, and are immensely profitable. They are of average feature length, and usually consist of a slight variation on an easily recognisable theme, such as the Western, the thriller, the bike picture etc. The plot is an excuse to get 'em off and get it on. An average reel will feature several straight heterosexual couplings, often in an unlikely setting, such as the Captain having it off with a stewardess in the plane's cockpit (*The Daisy Chain*); female masturbating scene; a Lesbian love scene; and the variations – cunnilingus and fellatio rampant or dormant or whatever, the introduction of a 'foreign object', usually a loudly buzzing vibrator, plus the occasional orgy.

Renewing his attack on the sex education film *Growing Up*, Lord Longford said it was positively insisted in the commentary that sexual intercourse between teenagers was perfectly in order.

> I refuse to believe that teachers and parents of this country are going to allow such depraved and depraving medicine to be administered in the schools. (Cheers).

The American films have many unfortunate characteristics in common. All the women are immediately available, no matter how unprepossessing the man, and invariably have earth-shattering orgasms, usually before a count of ten. This is semaphored by a standard routine of eye rolling, lip licking and cerebral moaning. They all have large breasts, which in the older films especially are no longer as God designed them; the new nickname for Hollywood is Silicone City. Most of the women are bisexual and a lesbian scene appears to be mandatory – presumably to assuage the threat to male virility.

The men have short hair cuts, are not young and are single-mindedly intent on increasing the number of notches on their bedposts. They treat their women as sexual objects, which is an attitude depicted as being both appropriate and welcomed by the ladies in question. Their lovemaking habits are peculiar – they are great tit-suckers, show dire signs of distress during orgasm and often keep their socks on.

All the sex scenes are quite obviously faked. Penetration is achieved either off camera or with cunning rapidity. No erect penises: the management's scissors intervene every time there's too much of this or when that's too obvious. Although there is more flesh and hair on view than usual, presumably to aid the memory, it really is all in the mind.

The Viscount Eccles, Paymaster-General and Minister responsible for the Arts, said that it was faintly possible that in time the inhabitants of Westminster might get used to copulating in the streets like dogs or pigeons, but not tomorrow morning. (See House of Lords Debate.)

The sex act is frequently equated with violence. At its most ludicrous this leads to an epic like *Sisters in Leather,* where our heroes, the local Hell's Angels, 'tame', i.e. rape, a gang of motor-bike-riding lesbians; yes, they actually do ride off together on their bikes. At its most obscene this results in the sickness of *The Ravager,* in which our hero can't get no satisfaction unless he masturbates while watching couples making love and then blowing them up in a grand succession of climaxes.

All the films are thoroughly dated in their attitudes, being located in some suburban middle American nightmare where doing what comes naturally is not only a right but a duty. Far from Vietnam indeed. The dialogue is ripe or rather putrid, the production slap-dash, with glaring continuity errors, and the whole is accompanied by repetitive music from the sound library. One of the few redeeming features is that many of the actors keep reappearing in each other's films, and have thus built up an atmosphere akin to amateur rep., with the fun being to see who is banging who this time around. The prize for prima donna of the bedroom must undoubtedly go to a lady called Marsha Jordan, who appears in film after film. She is an overripe blonde, complete with watermelon breasts and false eyelashes, and has reached climax in such roles as a divorcee, an Indian squaw, an air hostess, Catherine the Great and Lady Godiva.

Most of the films mimic, unashamedly and incompetently, the big Hollywood productions. Any humour is unintentional, any editing, lighting or direction is fortuitous.

The one exception is Russ Meyer, one of the first skin flic makers.

He is a consummate technician, directing, photographing and editing himself (his wife often does the scripts), and doing so with great and enjoyable panache (*vide Cherry, Harry and Raquel, How Much Loving Does a Normal Couple Need?, Good Morning and Goodbye* and the full length version of *Vixen*). Interestingly his films are not explicit—no genitals for instance—and they are often intentionally droll and whimsical. But generally the reflection these sex films cast on American society is saddening.

The handful of European sex films is generally superior: often they are not exploitation films at all in their home countries. The Swedish *To Ingrid My Love, Lisa* has virtually no sex at all; the Danish *I, a Woman* is well made and has a star performance from Essy Persson; the Italian co-production *Venus,* based on Sacher-Masoch's *Venus in Furs* is beautifully photographed; *Philosophy in the Boudoir* has Christopher Lee as the narrator and a genuinely black air of perversity and despair; and the French *Giselle* is simply a good film, with a really beautiful heroine, Nathalie Vernier. And the Classics sometimes unearth a find like Robbe-Grillet's *Trans-Europe Express* and Sjoman's *491*.

Of the American films *Starlet, Wild Gypsies, Hotspur, Baby Vickie, Cat Games* and *The Animal* are above average and have some worthwhile features, such as excellent location shooting in *Wild Gypsies*. *Submission* is a very strange film, evidently much cut; brilliantly photographed in black and white, it is about a girl who has an obsession for sweets. *The Secret Sex Lives of Romeo and Juliet* won a prize at Cannes for the best erotic film, and is very funny if you are in the mood. And there's the aforementioned Russ Meyer ... and that's about it; all that's left is the ones with the nice titles, like *The Scream of the Butterfly* and *The Diary of Knockers McCalla*: terrible films both.

Lord Longford, who had just completed a tour of strip clubs and a study of sex films and pornography, said he had received more than 1,000 letters, some containing many signatures, about his campaign.

The above is a reasonably accurate assessment of the films. They are not pornographic as are those currently being shown in Sweden, Denmark, Holland and America. The proposed new legislation on cinema clubs is quite plainly a political gambit, designed to pacify the distraught backwoodsmen from whom the two major parties are supposed to derive their strength. I seriously doubt whether Lord Longford has seen any of these films in a club cinema; if he had, he would realise that he is inveighing against an audience of his peers. The clubs are merely a symptom of a sex obsessed society: ask any Dane, or take a look at some adverts ... If the good Lord really wants to get down to the nitty gritty of sex, he should try listening to Aretha Franklin singing 'Pullin' '. But that's another story.

Discussing stag films proper, the American Inquiry into Pornography reported in their 70-year history:

> Production has changed only in form, not in sexual content. Stag films feature a full range of sexual activity, including fellatio, cunnilingus, and mutual masturbation. Because pornography historically has been thought to be primarily a masculine interest, the emphasis in stag films seems to represent the preferences of the middle-class American male. Thus, male homosexuality and bestiality are relatively rare, while lesbianism is rather common. In recent years, there has been an increased emphasis on group sex, usually three or four individuals, but as many as seven have been noted in a single film.

Hard-core blue films, then, have a diminishing number of taboos to exploit, notably sodomy, juveniles, clearly defined cocks in cunts, spurting semen and the deviation area where whips and women pale before the new pulling power of man's best friend, the dog (pigs are another feature of the bestiality business with 'funnies' reserved for sheep lovers).

These sorts of picture are advertised through that simplest of oral contacts, the whisper, either from a tout on a street corner or the mate on the factory floor. They tend to be shown on private walls or in garden sheds. They are the nitty gritty of what we understand by the pornographic film and remain illegal.

A FEW FRAMES:

1. Pornographic film maker: 'Look, when you're going to shoot your load withdraw immediately and hold it so's I can focus my close-up lens and when you hear the camera whirring again I want

you to come all over her right tit.' (Documentary *Naughty* as quoted in *Scorpio* magazine.)

2. Re the new style stag-porn stars (and see *Underground*): 'The actors have a wonderful sense of detachment, in that they're faking out the squares.' Dr William Simon.

'I may have a sore twat after working a lot, but otherwise my career doesn't affect a private relationship.' A stag star.

'I quit the business, because I was getting ripped off. I had to make it with guys I wouldn't look twice at, let alone go to bed with. The final straw was the time I was supposed to do three fuck scenes in one day, and on a filthy bed at that. The least they could have done was provide clean sheets, right!' A stag star.

3. 'On the eve of the second and last Wet Dream Festival in Amsterdam, sponsored by *Suck,* the European sex-paper, Al Goldstein, editor of the New York sexpaper *Screw,* sat in a super-luxury apartment in the middle of the city, with a party going on around him. Pneumatic ladies with henna hair. Light sculptures with glow from within. Inverted tubas, zebra skins and polar bear rugs. A colour movie of two blonde ladies sharing a dildo, without using their hands ...' Robert Greenfield in *Rolling Stones.*

4. 'Donna and Ralph after meeting go to "UNCLE'S" castle where a party is in full swing and learn that this particular party is "UNCLE'S" wake. They find "UNCLE" in his upstairs room sitting in his usual place on his stage apparently dead. But he starts to move and talk as though he were a robot and explains that nothing has changed but everything is to go on as usual. Donna and Ralph perform their sex act before "UNCLE'S" dead gaze. Downstairs the party guests are enjoying a modern Roman orgy in which two chained women acting as lions attempt to eat a young girl who is spread nude against a fireplace. Periodically as the clock strikes, each couple leaves to perform in front of "UNCLE" and there they receive a substantial check which "UNCLE" calls "THE TOY BOX" ... Suddenly "UNCLE" appears and tells them that he is from an alien world, collecting humans to sell them on his planet "Arcon". The Arcons devour human brains to experience human depravity. "UNCLE" used the castle and the parties to find the most depraved humans for his purpose. Donna disappears from sight and while Ralph looks on she is transformed into an Arcon. At the same time

"UNCLE'S" face disappears and Donna confesses that she is "UNCLE" and has been using Ralph to find the needed human brains for her planet. While she is telling him that he is under hypnosis and will not remember a thing the castle begins to DISSOLVE with the guests in it screaming frantically and trying to escape. And soon there is nothing but a quiet hillside where the castle once stood.' Publicity for *The Toy Box*, a club film.

5. 'Judge Paul W. LaPrade, in the county Superior Court of the State of Arizona on December 8, 1969, case No. 228092, rendered an opinion that *I am Curious* (*Yellow*) was obscene. This was the case of National General Corporation *v.* Mummert, Sheriff of Maricopa County. As to the context of this film, ruled not obscene in New York and New Jersey, Judge LaPrade says:

(*a*) A few minutes after being introduced to Borje by her father, Lena takes him into her room where they commenced an all-night love scene. Their nude bodies were graphically depicted, head to toe, caressing while standing up, on their knees, kissing her breasts and finally lying on their backs, tired and pensive. She tells him he is number 24, but the first 19 were no fun. He lies on top of her in the morning for the obvious purpose of more intercourse. After they leave, father urinates in the wash basin.

(*b*) Later that day Lena and Borje engage in a non-violent protest against monarchy in front of the Royal Palace in broad daylight, she takes off her panties, they straddle the balustrade, she sitting on him. The Swedish national anthem plays as they copulate in an explicit and graphic manner.

(*c*) On retreat, Lena reads a sex manual depicting various positions of sexual intercourse. They were clearly shown on the screen.

(*d*) On the grass at retreat, Borje tosses Lena to the ground and he performs oral-genital acts (cunnilingus). They make love in the nude, pubic areas and genitals in full view. She caresses and kisses his penis and simulates fellatio. He caresses her genitals.

(*e*) In the crotch of a large and ancient tree they experiment for a good sexual intercourse position. Trousers of each are then removed and he mounts her in the tree. Intercourse is explicit and certain.

(*f*) They struggle in a shallow pond. The scene closes with Borje nude on top of Lena, obviously having carnal knowledge.

(*g*) Back at the ranch house, Lena and Borje again disrobe, struggle in the nude in full view. Pubic areas at close up, and he takes her from the rear as they engage in either violent sexual intercourse or sodomy. They retire to the next room on the bare floor, still nude, flat on her back with loins entangled. Intercourse is clear, open and obvious.

(*h*) The fantasy of her dream depicts her twenty-three lovers tied to a tree as Borje approaches. After gunning him down she solemnly takes out her knife, unbuttons his pants, pulls them down and emasculates his genitals.

(*i*) The movie closed with Lena and Borje standing nude in full view facing camera while the hospital attendants delouse them.

As quoted in *The Report of the Commission on Obscenity and Pornography*.

6. 'The trouble with the censor is that he worries if a girl has cleavage. He should worry if she hasn't any.' Marilyn Monroe.

(N.B. film violence will be dealt with under *Violence*).

COLE: Dr Martin is a plant geneticist who has recently specialised in sex education through the Institute for Sex Education and Research, of which he is a founder member, and for whom he produced the film, *Growing Up*. He works with Dr Phillip Cauthery, whose main interest is in preventive medicine and psychosexuality and they collaborated on an excellent book *The Fundamentals of Sex* (W. H. Allen, 1971) that received hardly any publicity.

Dr Cole is lecturer in genetics at the University of Aston, was Chairman of the Birmingham Group of the Abortion Law Reform Association and a founder member of the Birmingham Brook Advisory Centre, the Birmingham Pregnancy Advisory Service and the Calthorpe Nursing Home, which specialises in legal abortions. Dr Cole's methods have brought ridicule and moral disapproval upon him, notably from Mrs Mary Whitehouse. In early 1972, he was at the centre of another controversy when he used women to attempt to help overcome impotence in men by putting the willing ladies in bed with the willing but incompetent men – a practice not unknown in social history and one that can give good results.

CUNNILINGUS: and *Fellatio* are hardly perversions, even if they can become obsessions. Most people find the idea of mouth-genital contact stimulating. Oral sex is probably the most widely exploited area of erotic contact and is ideally suited to all kinds of pornography, as it can be tactfully shown (in soft-core) or be quite explicit (in hard-core). Nearly all blue movies (see *Cinema*) feature fellatio (mouth-penis stimulation) and a lot focus on it as the main activity. Since pornography is male-orientated, fellatio is more commonly featured than cunnilingus although lesbian type material obviously utilises the erotic potentialities. Soixante-neuf (69), or mutual oral sex, is actually not so common in pornography, partly because it is more difficult to show with any detail, partly because sexual activity is usually shown to be something performed by one (or more) on another—not a reciprocal experience, which is what sex more often is in real life situations. Fellatio, and in notably all-girls productions cunnilingus, are ideal pornographic material because, like sado-masochism they are fantasy situations of infinite sexual satisfaction being performed on someone whom the reader/viewer can associate with. Oral sex is often declared illegal because it is considered unnatural.

DESTRUCTION ORDERS: 90 per cent of current censorship of sex books and magazines in this country is by means of destruction orders. Issued under Section 3 of the Obscene Publications Act (1959), they are a way of censoring sex material at the point of sale rather than the point of publication. As such, their effectiveness implies some restraint on the part of both the publishers and the police. On the part of the publishers because, as professionals, the last thing they want is a show trial, so that they don't fight destruction orders, brought before a magistrate's court. On the part of the police, because they choose to prosecute the bookseller and not the publisher of the book. (See also *Obscene Publications Act* for full discussion of the legal aspects of obscenity and pornography).

DIRTIEST SHOW IN TOWN: began in 1968/9 as an off-off Broadway show at the Café La Mama. Writer and director Tom Eyen has said of it:

> The original conception was sexuality, not pollution. I wanted to take the masculine-feminine syndrome and destroy it ... I wanted a show that would push revue into another dimension ... the underground theatre in New York works physical because it has no money. When we get elaborate, we fail.'

John Ford of *Time Out* gave *Show* one of the few reviews to look beyond the nudity when it arrived in London in May 1971:

> The cast take their clothes off twice. The first episode illustrates the confusion of love and sex. A woman and a man are romantically infatuated when they see each other. They make love-boom-boom-boom-boom-boom-boom-bang! – and it's all over. They've got nothing to say to each other. They hated it. They go their separate ways to do it all again with somebody else. The second episode is a superb send-up of the New York ad-man's 'beautiful people' set, an absurd, emotionless gang-bang. But that's only a fraction of an hour-and-half which explores the desperate search for love in a city that seems to deny everything but sex and thinking dirty.

Like all revues, *Show* has developed and changed. They put a lot more emphasis on pollution after a while. A tighter and tougher

Oh, Calcutta!? Or just another *Oh, Calcutta!* freed from the awesome responsibility to be deliberately erotic, able to use nudity as simply a part of the theatrical armoury? *Show* lies mid-way between the glossy, purposeless eroticism of *Oh, Calcutta!* which just wasn't very erotic and the deliberate use of nudity and sex on stage for political purposes in *Che* (never seen in England and charged with obscenity in New York). *Show* is more relaxed and more pointed than either: the play is really the thing and not the thing the play. That didn't stop every critic in Britain rushing to comment on how turned on or not turned on they were, a disgraceful performance, even if we should be used to it. As Bradford Riley, one of the American cast who came to London with *Show*, wrote:

> My hair is intact and I am not shaken by the simple idiocy of sexually maladjusted London daily critics. They merely want to be teased as the daily papers tease and use women, as though the pleasure in it lies in knowing that IT exists—IT meaning sex. We should all know by now how IT is used to gain ends ... Yet it is this innocent display of IT that rocked the contemporary world of London. Meaning, of course, that London would rather not face the bull by the tail but would rather dress the bull up, rather sexily, in a scantily-clad nightdress, in order to entice us into coitus union with more bullshit.

Paradoxically, it is exactly all the bullshit which has enabled a basically pointed, but very American revue, most of whose satire is lost on Londoners, to run for over a year in the West End under the guise of being a sex play.

EROTIC ART: Many people take pornography to be an artistic product, and judge it as such. There is confusion between erotic art and pornographic art, and some writers on pornography have tended to regard eroticism as the art and pornography as the commercial craft. Pornography, in its wider sense, certainly can be regarded as a business, perhaps analogous to advertising (see *Exploitation*) but, like advertising, it can also be regarded as an artistic genre.

Unfortunately the so-called liberals in sexology have been as culpable in causing confusion as have the reactionaries. Leaders in this have been the Drs Kronhausen (also see *Pornography*), whose views have influenced other writers who take their cue from the Kronhausens.

Others however have disagreed strongly with the Kronhausens' attitude to pornographic art. Shortly after the Kronhausens' book based on their Copenhagen exhibition was published (*Erotic Art*, W. H. Allen, 1971), the author of another book (*Pornography or Art*, Words and Pictures), Poul Gerhard, took them to task but without mentioning them by name:

> In 1968, Sweden held its first exhibition of pornographic art, but unfortunately the organiser failed to acknowledge the word pornography. Instead they described the exhibition as a display of erotic art, and an attempt was made to distinguish between erotic art and pornography on the basis of pornography being harmful speculation, while erotic art is a creditable artform. This distinction simply preserved the confusion of ideas clearly demonstrated in legislation which, on the one hand, allows art of erotic content, but, on the other hand, forbids pornography.

Pornography, for Gerhard, is

> a depiction of one of the most beautiful sides of human life, a reflection of, and an ode to, erotic enjoyment ... Pornographic art is a term used to describe art which shows erotic life, is associated with it or is erotically motivated.

Gerhard reiterates the essential point:

> Any art based on economic speculation is, quite simply, bad art. This applies to pornographic art as to any other. But today most psychologists reject the postulate that pornography, even

when it is artistically inferior, is harmful. Bad art, including bad pornographic art, is merely trivial.

The dispute emphasises the confusion between terms. In actuality the choice made by the Kronhausens for their *Erotic Art* is remarkably similar to Gerhard's for his *Pornography or Art*. Little-known works by great masters, such as Courbet's realism (his 'Torso' is so realistic and uncompromising it wouldn't be out of place in a Soho bookshop); Rembrandt's domestic scenes (many of which give us the added delight of guessing whether the recumbent lady is the artist's wife or his housekeeper); Toulouse-Lautrec's sketches and Picasso's celebrated drawings and paintings, share the honours with works of amazing sensitivity by lesser artists whose Muse seemed only to visit in states of high erotic tension: Willy Jaekel, Thomas Rowlandson, Guilio Romano, Hans von Aachen and the anonymous Roman artists who decorated the walls of Pompeii, miraculously preserved by Vesuvian lava, all will be remembered more for their odd masterpieces of pornographic art than for anything else. The number of artists who devoted their entire energies to the celebration of the erotic are few: Felicien Rops, the Marquis von Bayros, Beardsley (though somewhat overrated: his only real contribution to pornography was in his illustration to Aristophanes' *Lysistrata* and in his uncompleted novel *Under the Hill*); Clovis Trouille and the nameless illustrators who flourished in those great eras of pornography, Ancient Greece and Rome, eighteenth-century Japan, Restoration and Renaissance Europe and the late nineteenth century in England and France.

Today pornographic art is very healthy. Allen Jones, Bertrand, Hans Bellmer, Ernst Fuchs, Rolf Bock, Otto Dressler, Eberhard Schlotter, Heimrad Prem, Lothard Fischer and others are all exploring sexuality with a frankness that is quite refreshing. Sometimes the work is erotic, simply or surrealistically, sometimes it is simply pornographic.

One movement that couldn't have existed without dear old Sigmund Freud is the so-called 'Cop Art' school – Cop being short for Copulation, and the unwritten manifesto assents to Freud's insistence that everything in life is erotically motivated. Freud's errant disciple Wilhelm Reich has influenced other artists, principally American, who utilise the Reichian theory of orgasm relief (surrender to orgasm is the cure to all things, personal and political), to indulge in mystique-shattering things like plaster casts of erect phalluses and drawings of masturbating voluntary models. Cop Art is supposed to have started with the eroticism of America's Tom Wesselman, Britain's Allen Jones, Germany's Schreiber, Dressler, Prem, Fischer and the Austrian Fuchs, all of them born in the 1930s and thus still fairly young, and all associated with Cop Art.

The precursors of modern pornography were the Expressionists and Surrealists: of the first group, Max Beckmann, Ernst, Willy Geiger, Michael Fingersten, Walter Klemm and Joseph Steiner Ensor all produced pornographic works, some clandestinely (notably Ernst and Ensor) some openly; of the Surrealists, much of the works of Dali, Magritte and Wilhelm Freddie (who was actually imprisoned for an 'indecent' sculpture) had pornographic elements and was insidiously erotic.

EXPLOITATION: Until recently porn was very much a clandestine thing – in fact we might well suppose that a lot of its appeal lay precisely in the fact that it was clandestine. It's been argued, and very strongly, that if the veils of secrecy are removed from the porn business – as has happened in Denmark – a lot of the attraction disappears: the death of censorship means the death of pornography.

Like any industry, pornography is subject to certain market forces and to general marketing strategies. As a business it's odd, because basically it is concerned with consumer goods and yet it operates on the reverse of the usual maximum-exposure advertising sales principles of other products. Pornographic, unlike any other magazines, aren't concerned with image, with ad revenue or with variable content. Unlike supermarket goods, pornography isn't concerned with packaging, price competitiveness or any other enticements to the prospective buyer. Unlike industry or any steady business, it isn't concerned with long-term profitability but merely with immediate sales. With no open competition, prices are high, standards are low, advertising is unimportant (and, realistically, impossible), choice is dependent on the producers, there's no market research and no incentives to customers. In fact, in many ways pornography is a remarkably honest business: where it gets dirty is in promising more than it offers (more in the middle-core goods) and in the high returns for minimal expenditure. This business profile extends right across the soft-to-hard range of pornography. Certain more esoteric publications and 'intellectual pornography' are concerned with standards, but these aren't really part of the pornography industry.

What the industry does know very well, better than its counterparts in tobacco, confectionery or washing powders, is its customers. The market generally is amazingly constant and undemanding, non-fickle and docile. There are market trends, not so much in sales, but in content: a little while ago, leather and rubber gear staged a comeback from being a steady minority interest. Lesbianism has been coming up strong and, in the finer points of the trade, it's said that oral love is fighting a rearguard action against older-women-and-younger-men scenes. There are naturally familiar, timeless favourites that are evidenced in Pompeian frescoes as much as in lavatory graffiti today and have been the pornographer's standby: the US pornography commission's technical reporters found that, regardless of sex or medium of presentation, first every time was cunnilingus as an erotic theme; ordinary intercourse and group oral sex were runners-up, with fellatio, anal intercourse and nude heterosexual petting also figuring prominently. Slight variations from visual to literary pornography were interesting: nude females petting were more arousing in book form than in photographs, as was homosexual fellatio, but anal intercourse and partially-clad homosexual petting won hands down photographically. Of course, in hard-core porn *general* reactions such as these are precisely what aren't catered for – it's the way-out stuff that features strongly. In the American survey, sado-masochistic material came bottom all the time, but there's little doubt that it is a strong component of a lot of across-the-range porn. By far the strongest subject, especially in Danish porn, is bestiality; plastic macs, bondage, paedophilia and other obsessions are also well featured.

In pornography, it isn't ever one highly successful product that makes a fortune. The industry is geared to maximum production of as many items as possible. For the originator, there's infinite spin-off to be made from one photo session with sales to the hard-core men right down to the girlie mags. Hard-core porn is reckoned to make £10 millions a year in the UK and soft-core £100 millions; and this is nearly all on a vast number of different products, not one big seller. The better class medium-core books, for example, might sell 15,000 – and one firm, who sell their books by mail order and in sex shops only, claims considerably more. The nastier medium-core books probably do about 5,000. Magazine sales, as far as they're available, vary from 15,000 for the sort of pseudo-educational mags you see on bookstands to 250,000 for *Men Only*; with staffs to support, paid contributors and all the trappings of straight commercial magazines – including high print bills – these soft to medium-core productions need to sell more than an average paperback and a lot more than hard-core porn, with soft to medium-core prices rarely more than 50p a shot. Hard-core costs £1 upwards, sometimes as much as £10. Films cost £5–£15 for medium to hard-core flicks, coming from Scandinavia, the US and often home-produced. Soft-core films are on view at cinema clubs for something like 50p admission fee but they don't show explicit sexual activity. They aren't usually any the less erotic for it.

The actual market is less simple to define. As many observers have commented, a good proportion of men to be seen loitering around Soho shops are likely to be sociologists, reporters, rubber-neckers and disguised evangelists. There was a study of the clientele of porn shops in the US in 1970, but it doesn't reveal all that much:

> Over half were casually dressed, 26 per cent wore suits and ties, 13 per cent were blue-collar workers; the remainder were soldiers, students, tourists, hippies and clergymen.

A general finding that is notable, was that porn patrons were proportionally as disinterested as the average person in sado-masochism, paedophilia, bestiality and nonconsensual sex; this was in a survey of customers of the whole range of soft-to-hard-core porn, however. According to one source, there are four distinct types of 'punter', as the consumer is known: the straight hetero type looking for fantasy stimulus; the bondage type whose fantasy material must involve chains and straps; the transvestite, probably the smallest group; and the flag boys, or flagellists, by far the most diligent, demanding and persistent consumers in the market.

As with all consumer industries, the product is determined by the demands of the market and by a certain secondary creation of demand by the producers. The market is so consistent—indeed there is an intimate feedback process from consumer to producer via the retailer that must be the envy of IPC—that the whole process is, on the one hand, the satisfaction of a desperate need and, on the other, the usual exploitation of desires that cannot be satisfied on the open market. Clearly there is a need for pornography as a product and one wonders what the 'market' would do without it; one also wonders how much the 'market's' appetite is reinforced and consistently whetted by currently-available products, and just what sort of difference would come about if pornography ceased to be a back-street business and was marketed as a price more in keeping with the cost, rather than the scarcity value, of the contents.

FLEET STREET: The national Press is the public consciousness rather than conscience, in many ways. Its role in the pornography tragicomedy is some of the time as Everyman, some of the time as a Touchstone: various columns in various papers act as liberal/reactionary watchdogs while in all newspapers the coverage of stories and features dealing with sexual topics has very noticeably got more 'permissive'. The posh Sundays as well as the *Guardian* feel no compunction about four-letter words and coyness—an attribute that tends to reflect public acceptance of taboo topics—has broadened from vague references to 'intimacy with' and photos of bikini-clad starlets in the *News of the World* a couple of years ago to nipple-revealing nude models and quite frank reference to sex crimes (a good barometer of permissible language in the Press) in all today's popular Press. The Press, of course, is the most astute medium for gauging its readers' tolerance levels. The most successful papers are inevitably those that know their readers. In the matter of pornography, the papers have managed to mix with customary cleverness an inherent pornography of their own with an equally clever market-sensitive moral stance to the subject. The *News of the World* still manages to titillate by seeming shocked by immorality; the *Guardian* and *Observer* placate their intellectual middle-class readers by appearing terribly liberal and yet totally responsible; the *Sunday Express* has scandal on page 3 and John Gordon in the middle of the paper ranting against sex, drugs, and radicals; the *Sunday Times* colour supp has high-class erotica disguised as fashion photos (as do *Nova, Honey, Flair, Vogue* and even the teeny-bopper romance mags); all told, most newspapers manage to do their usual trick of satisfying the different readers' desires while agreeing with their prejudices and moral values.

The *Sun* is obviously the most notable example of the Press's attitude to pornography and it reveals a lesson about it. The lesson is that in reality pornography does not exist. The kind of photographs printed in the *Sun* today were called pornography just a few years ago; they are not pornography now. I suspect that any intelligent person examining a set of articles that he considers pornographic will, by the time he has waded through them, not consider them any such thing: the word will have lost all meaning because it is used simply to describe that which is outside moral acceptability – but that something which is always *just* outside. In other words, as soon as it becomes a reality – that is, when it comes within our real-life acquaintanceship – then we call it something else. The nudes in the *Sun* would have been pornography a few years ago because the average popular paper reader then would not be used to seeing sexy naked girls in the context of his morning paper (and not even, at that time, in most pin-up magazines); the nudes are not pornography now, because pornography is even today something that the average popular paper reader isn't used to seeing – perhaps a sexy-looking girl sucking the genital organs of another sexy-looking girl, or having sex with a dog, or being buggered by an ugly-looking man. The interesting speculation is what the situation will be like in a decade or so. If the *Sun* is then including photographs of what we now call pornography then it's difficult to think what we will then be able to label as pornography. I suspect it simply won't exist, or rather it will finally be admitted that it never has existed except in the mind. Pornography is that unknown something that is just more extreme than current morality permits – which is why the Victorians were obsessed by it, of course. (Their Press wasn't very different from ours, incidentally; nineteenth-century family journals were full of letters discussing things like corporal punishment that were transparently sadistic, and sexually so.) Since it is just beyond the accepted norm, it not only provides society with the necessary guidance on what is permitted and what isn't, it is always just beyond people's actual experience. And it is these two areas precisely that the Press is concerned with: news is supposed to inform on the unknown, features and comment to reflect on the state of society. That is why Fleet Street is in the perfect position to respond to pornography and why if we ever want to know what is pornography we should read the news pages for sexual events and the candour with which they are reported (compare any sex crime report a decade ago with one recently); read the features to find out what sexual topics it is acceptable to talk about, read the editorial comment (adjusting to the political stance of the paper in question) to get the 'average' enlightened attitude on such things as obscenity – and look at the photographs and adverts to see just how much eroticism is considered offensive.

The Press's most famous trick must be 'isn't it shocking, now read on'. Herewith one example:

> There is even an advertisement for a Coital Cook Book. The sexiest cook-book ever published, runs the advertisement, Should be required reading for anybody who wants to add a taste of sensuality to an intimate occasion. There is a recipe for flaming virgin, which consists largely of cherries, ice-cream and brandy. Even jewellers are now going in for pornography. At the Electrum Gallery in South Molton Street, London, wealthy rakes could recently buy such works of art as silver rings in the shape of a penis at £14 and a pair of silver key rings at £52, one in the form of a woman, the other shaped as a man so that the two can be interlocked in sexual intercourse positions ... For more modest purses at the 'Happy End' sex shop in High Holborn, London, there is a lampshade at £2.95. When the light is switched on, the figure of a nude girl appears on the shade with her legs apart and her pubic hair showing.

(The *Sunday People* 13.2.72).

Wealthy rakes, gosh!

G STRING: The G string and the nipple cap were symbols of latent modesty and legal restraint in that ancient pursuit called striptease, a feature not only of Soho, but a surprising number of British towns including Bournemouth. From 1964 onwards, they were no longer necessary. Hence the G string symbolises the milder end of the erotic market, frequently referred to rather loosely as pornography—soft-core, for those who see it as a drug.

The wraps off the body are paralleled by the wraps off words, and the 1950s was the last decade to trade in cheeky hints of flesh-sweaters, cleavage, wind up the skirt. Since then, it has been a simple matter of nudity, preferably total, and a large increase in verbal sexual description. First of the major taboos to tumble was probably lesbianism and open sale appetisers include well-known people in the nude, a spot of fetishism and sexy ads (see *Underground*).

'Strengths' of material according to the *Sunday People* inquiry are

> *Soft porn*. The mildest category. There is no explicit sex act but it is suggested. Nudity is shown, but there is no display of genitals. *Hard porn*. Full frontal nudity, genitalia—both male and female included. The sex act is explicitly portrayed and practices usually regarded as deviant are shown. *Super-hard porn*. Nothing barred. Sex orgies featured in great detail. Animals and human beings shown in bestial association. Mostly in full colour and specialising in maximum colour.

Under item two, a number of American publications like *Ankh* and *Quickie*, with English imitators, feature every orifice and combination (human) in massive detail but make the one stipulation that the male penis must be unaroused. I suppose this is some legal restraint rather than lack of energy on the part of the models.

Open sale English magazines produce their frankest pictures in the name of sex education but the mass distribution monthly girlie magazines which have pushed simple female nudity farthest are *Playboy, Penthouse, Mayfair* and, above all, the new-style *Men Only*. These all now favour (i.e. the law doesn't forbid) female pubic hair. Old-fashioned in the latter respect are the non-glossy cheaper weeklies like *Parade*. No pubic hair.

GIRODIAS:

We must accept love and lust as complementary movements, and not as incompatible elements. We must discover desire as the source of all the positive actions in our life, and stop opposing every natural instinct and every pleasure-giving activity. That result cannot be achieved without a series of mental shocks and convulsions. My sincere, if paradoxical, wish is that my activity as a publisher shall have helped to destroy a few taboos, and to clear the air.

Maurice Girodias, half-French and half-English, his father a Manchester business man, is the now famous founder of Olympia Press, started in 1953. And his thoughts above are quoted in Montgomery Hyde's solid historical résumé *A History of Pornography*. Girodias has been shocking and convulsing ever since, with a series of engaging and profitable titles, both big works of art and hot works of sex. The list up to 1964, and therefore before the massive extension of licence to print, includes the introduction of such writers to the English-speaking public as Samuel Beckett (*Watts, Molloy*), Jean Genet (*Our Lady of the Flowers, The Thief's Journal*), Vladimir Nabokov (*Lolita*), William Burroughs (*The Naked Lunch*) and J. P. Donleavy (*The Ginger Man*).

His other titles include *Who Pushed Paula?*, *White Thighs, The Chariot of Flesh, The Story of O, Whipsdom,* and *The Sexual Life of Robinson Crusoe*. In addition he has reprinted such sexual classics as the Earl of Rochester's *Sodom* and Aubrey Beardsley's *Under the Hill*.

Much more recently he has been taken to task by The *Sunday People* under their banner headline of 'Seven Erotic Minutes for 1,000 City Secretaries'. 16–26-year-old girls were reputed to be swarming into shops to purchase such titles as this one, *Seven Erotic Minutes*, a vigorous, well-written piece which leaves no hole unscrewed and appears on semi-open sale in a smart new jacket at the bargain price of 60p.

GUILT BY ASSOCIATION: a favourite argument among the moralists. Depends on a sort of 'bluff man's blindness' which makes it the perfect argument for the silent majority. Originally used by Charles Keating, the dissenting commissioner on the US Commission Report and Chairman of Citizens for Decent Literature (see *US Commission*); then adapted for this country by Mary Whitehouse (see *Mary*) who devotes a long section of her recent autobiography to endorsing one Ray Gauer, Keating's emissary to Europe. (It's surprising Keating even believes Europe still exists, so convinced is he of the imminent collapse of Western civilisation.)

The police also believe firmly in guilt by association. Indeed it is the police, making available to the anti-pornographers material they would never make available to the rest of us, who provide the whole case for it. This, stated simply, is a statistical one. In a large number of sex crimes, sex books or sex material are found on or near the suspect. In some cases, suspects have even confessed that reading a particular sex book or magazine excited them to commit the crime. The argument, of course, is double-edged. You can argue with the anti-pornographers that this 'common sense' and 'practical experience' (always fondly referred to by people whose evidence is shaky on its own account) proves sex materials lead to sex crime. You could also, we suppose, argue the reverse. Perhaps if sex criminals were abolished, obscenity and pornography would vanish also. Guilt by association is illogical – because A apparently preceded and was linked with B, therefore A must have been the cause of B. None of the real questions are answered: is there some fundamental sickness in sex criminals which motivates them both to read pornography and commit sex crimes? If there were no pornography (a legal impossibility – rather, if pornography went underground), would such people lose a valuable safety valve and in fact become yet more unstable? And so on.

HISTORY: The crime of creating or distributing 'obscene' sexual materials is of relatively recent origin in Anglo-American law. In England, it was held authoritatively as late as 1705 that such materials were not indictable at common law, although 'obscene libel' was found punishable in England through judicial decision in 1727. The first legislation in England authorising the prosecution of obscene materials was enacted in 1824, and covered public exposure of obscene books or prints. England did not enact legislation generally prohibiting the distribution of obscenity until Lord Campbell's Act in 1857, and a broad definition was not formulated for application through this legislation until the decision of Queen *v.* Hicklin 1868.

In the United States, the distribution of obscenity never became firmly established as a common-law offence, although there were one or two common-law prosecutions in the 1800s. Only one colony—Massachusetts—enacted an obscenity statute, the other colonies apparently left the subject unregulated. The first state statute was enacted in Vermont in 1821. The first federal statute, prohibiting the importation of pictorial obscene matter, was enacted in 1842. Obscenity was first prohibited in the mails in 1865.

Nor were the earliest obscenity prohibitions directed toward explicit sexual materials as such. The crime of obscenity started in both England and the United States as a crime in which sexual matter was incorporated in materials which directly attacked religious institutions and beliefs. The earliest prosecutions all pertained to sexual works which were condemned for their explicit anti-religious content. It was not until after 1850 that a distinct offence of publishing explicit sexual material—unconnected with any expressed anti-religious content—fully evolved in the United States and England. The primary forces behind the ultimate creation of these prohibitions upon sexual materials appear, moreover, to have been religious ones.

The following paragraphs briefly summarise the steps in the legal development of the offence of obscenity which led to the emergence in the late 19th century of a prohibition upon published sexual explicitness. The development and elaboration of obscenity law after the late 19th century is described in succeeding Sections of this Report which deal with present legal doctrines.

EARLY BEGINNINGS IN ENGLAND: Censorship for political and religious reasons dates back at least to Greek and Roman times. In both cultures, however, sexual licentiousness was tolerated in drama (a principal means of popular entertainment) and was often combined with religious themes. During medieval times, bawdiness was apparently quite acceptable in ballads (again, frequently mixed with religious themes) and even in religious works. The *Exeter Book*, for example, a largely devotional work which is the earliest example of Anglo-Saxon literature, contains explicit sexual riddles which were collected by a monk.

The printing of books increased greatly in England in the 15th century. Royal censorship began in England in 1538 through a licensing system established by Henry VIII. Like earlier manifestations of governmental censorship in other cultures, however, English censorship at this time was not directed toward sexual content, but only against seditious and heretical works. Subsequently, the strong influence of Puritanism in England in the first half of the 17th century led to authorisation in 1605 of proceedings against the use of profanity by actors on stage and the total abolition of the play houses by Parliament in 1642. The licensing system may have been used to prohibit sexual explicitness during this time. After the Restoration in 1660, however, licensing was again limited to suppressing sedition and heresy in printed works, and the play houses were revived.

The only prosecution in England prior to the 18th century which nearly related to what was later deemed to be 'obscenity' was King *v.* Sedley in 1663. Sir Charles Sedley, an intimate of Charles II, became drunk with two friends at a tavern. They climbed to the balcony of the tavern, which overlooked Covent Garden, and removed their clothes. Sedley thereupon gave a speech which included profanities and poured bottles of urine down upon his audience. A riot followed. Sedley was given a substantial fine and committed to jail for a week for breaking the peace. The case is often referred to as the first reported obscenity case, apparently because it showed that common-law courts would, even in the absence of a statute, penalise conduct which was grossly offensive to the public. Sedley's case, however, did not concern the distribution of sexual materials, but involved both physical assault upon others and the public broadcasting of profanity and nudity upon unwilling recipients. It has little direct relationship with the offence of distributing sexual works to consenting recipients which was later evolved by the law.

The end of the 17th century in England brought the beginning of long-term governmental concern with the morals of the public in the sexual area which culminated in the Victorian period. Puritan repression of stage plays was renewed. A Society for the Reformation of Manners, which blacklisted persons guilty of 'vice', was formed under Royal patronage and Queen Anne issued a proclamation denouncing vice. On the other hand, the Licensing Act was allowed to lapse by Parliament in 1695 because of practical considerations. This, coupled with the spread of literacy and the increased popularity of reading, led to a new class of 'popular' literature which often had sexual content and which caused concern because of its appeal to lower-class readers. Nevertheless, in 1708 a man named Read, author of a book called, *The Fifteen Plagues of a Maidenhead,* was acquitted. The book was held by the court to be 'bawdy stuff', but since it libelled no one, did not reflect upon the government and did not attack religion, it was held to be 'punishable only in the spiritual court'.

THE DEVELOPMENT OF THE ENGLISH LAW OF OBSCENITY: In the 1720s one Curl was prosecuted for 'obscene libel' in publishing a book entitled *Venus in the Cloister* or *The Nun in her Smock*. The judges were troubled by the Read decision and by the fact that, previously, the common law had not recognised as crimes acts which did not tend to a breach of the peace, as Curl's book did not. However, after several continuances a conviction was rendered in 1727. As shown by its titles, the work in issue in Curl's case was offensive not solely because of its sexual content, but also because of its anti-religious content. An early report of the case states that the court found there to be an offence because 'religion was part of the common law; and therefore whatever is an offence against that is evidently an offence against the common law.'

Eighteenth-century legal writers treated the offence of obscene libel created by Curl as an offence against God, and obscenity cases which followed Curl's similarly limited themselves to sexual material in the context of anti-religious works. In fact, some of the sexually very explicit books and pamphlets of the type often referred to today as hard-core pornography circulated quite freely in England throughout the 18th century, apparently because their lack of anti-religious content kept them outside the law's proscription.

Early in the 19th century, the common law appears to have evolved by degrees in England to the extent that it began to be applied in some cases to prohibit purely sexual works even though they did not attack or libel religious institutions. It has been estimated that there were about three obscenity prosecutions per year in England between 1802 and 1857. Obscenity legislation was first enacted in England as part of the Vagrancy Act of 1824, which prohibited exposing an obscene book or print in public places. In 1853, a statute, apparently aimed at French postcards, was passed to prohibit the importation of obscene materials and in 1857 the so-called Lord Campbell's Act was enacted, generally prohibiting the dissemination of obscenity.

Lord Campbell's Act did not contain a definition of what was deemed 'obscene', but in 1868, in Queen *v.* Hicklin, an authoritative judicial definition was adopted. The Hicklin case involved an anti-religious pamphlet with sexual content, entitled *The Confessional Unmasked,* showing the depravity of the Roman Priesthood, the iniquity of the confessional and the questions put to females in confession. The opinion of the court, however, did not expressly limit itself to material with anti-religious content. It held instead that the test of obscenity was

> whether the tendency of the matter charged with obscenity is to deprave and corrupt those whose minds are open to such immoral influences, and into whose hands a publication of this sort may fall.

Hicklin thus made it clear in England, for the first time, that publications might be prohibited as 'obscene' solely on the grounds of their sexual content, and not because of their attack upon the government or upon religious institutions. (From the *Report of the US Commission on Obscenity and Pornography*, 1970.)

HOUSE OF LORDS DEBATE: Famous debate on 21 April 1971, during which Lord Longford first revealed his plans for a personal inquiry into pornography. The 'debate that launched a thousand quips'—among them, '"Lord Porn", amid the alien porn'—but included not a single statistic. In essence the Lords debate was a re-run or repeat of the permissive *v.* reactionary battle that had been fought out all through the 1960s in the law courts.

By 1967 and the *Last Exit to Brooklyn* Trial, the courts had clearly come out on the side of permissiveness and all attempts to turn the clock back (see the *Oz* Trial) were more or less doomed to failure. Hence the resort of the reactionaries to extra-legal measures. A Lords debate is in many ways the establishment version of a sit-in or demo, and contains many of the same ingredients: muddled politics, calls for direct action, a burning sense of moral purpose and lively criticism of the police. It is also, and equally, the cockpit of a generation. So the Lords discussed not the state of pornography in this country, nor its nature, nor its effects, nor even whether or not it had 'increased', was increasing and ought to be diminished' (the Motion before the House), but, quite simply, how they themselves felt about it.

The results were predictably entertaining. No one had much first-hand experience of porn, although one or two Lords knew a lot about the situation in Egypt, thanks to the Second World War. Lord Ferrier said he enjoyed 'shall we say?—a measure of robust musical-hall type vulgarity', though he did 'not go to the cinema because everybody else smokes cigarettes ... and I smoke a pipe. I hardly ever go to the theatre because I cannot afford it. But through my family, I do have contact with the young.' Viscount Masserene and Ferrard had discovered 'completely bestial' literature on sale down the King's Road and Royal Avenue only because it had been brought to his attention by 'foreign tourists', who doubtless ring the Lords all the time about such things. Lord Roberthall read the *Arabian Nights* in Sir Richard Burton's translation at Oxford where his college kept it in a locked cupboard in a locked room—either because it was dirty or because they realised it was worth a few bob. Lord Maelor spoke only after receiving 'a letter from an unknown lady in Caernarvon' but didn't hesitate, on this evidence, to pledge the support of the Welsh people as a whole to Lord Longford.

Lord Strange stated, appropriately enough, that he lived 'in a hut high up on a mountain', never saw television and 'hardly ever' read the newspapers. Only Viscount Norwich admitted that 'I too have stood breast high "amid the alien porn"', and only Viscount Ingleby was prepared to go one further and admit what it actually did to him: 'I know that it drags me down,' he said, 'I know that it pulls my whole personality down; I know that it saps my moral strength and leaves me feeling in a sort of vacuum.' All of which sounds less like reading than masturbation.

Intellectually, the debate was a farce. In talking about pornography no two people, it seemed, were talking about the same thing. Most Lords would have agreed with Lord Beswick: 'I want to curb those who seek simply to exploit the sexual instinct for commercial gain.' But why? Because he hated capitalism? The suspicion lingered that pornography was just the banner under which the Lords were mounting an attack on a much wider range of things. 'Pornography', Lord Eccles Minister for the Arts, said 'is the ugly child of the permissive society' (which we are delighted to note is married):

> Kidnapping has begun here; universities are disrupted by quite small numbers of their students; many thousands of work people go out on strike against their better judgement; security guards are shot-up in daylight; and sections of the arts are polluted by pornographers.

In other words, sex has replaced Marx as the secret ingredient, the Brand X, forcing white out, forcing dirt in to the very fabric of our society. Or has it? According to Lord Ferrier, porn is just another of His agents:

> Is it promoted by the powers of anti-Christ? I believe there is every reason to think that it is. Some time ago, a definite link between international Communism and the distribution to adolescents of certain pornographic material was established by a specific case in Scotland.

In Scotland? Can it be that they really *want* Scotland?

But it was Lord Longford who called the debate and Lord Longford's views that set its tenor. He wanted to 'curb down those who seek simply to exploit the sexual instinct for commercial gain' because he wanted to 'curb ... the sexual instinct'. The Lords were frightened of two things: modern society and ancient sexuality; an they were frightened on behalf of two groups: the poor/ignorant and the young. No one is going to admit they are frightened for themselves. On the contrary 'older people protect themselves against it by ignoring it because they have learned the wisdom of avoiding temptations which they find it difficult to resist', whereas the young 'are all too susceptible to the corrupting influence of the continuous contact' and may be drawn into 'a life of sexuality and lust' (Lord Nugent).

If only it was that easy. The young featured strongly throughout the debate from the 'unknown lady' from Wales who was 'grieved because of the terrible evil influence which this has on our youngsters' to Lord Longford who stated simply and terrifyingly: 'So far as I am concerned I would regard anybody who taught my children—or now, my grandchildren—to indulge in this pre-marital fornication as doing something utterly evil.'

Of course, nobody ever teaches anything of the kind. One of the most revealing things about the debate was the way in which Longford and his supporters regard the sexual instincts as something so compulsive, so impossible to resist, that to teach that sex is not wrong is the same as teaching that sex must be had at once, this minute, anywhere and everywhere—a vision taken to its final absurdity by Lord Eccles's description of the 'inhabitants of Westminster' who 'might get used to copulating in the streets like dogs or pigeons; but, my Lords, not tomorrow'.

The inhabitants, or at any rate, all the young ones and the 'lower IQ members' (Lord Clifford) can still be saved. Dogs and pigeons are presumably past it. Animals have all the fun.

But the last words on shock and age were surely said by Baroness Gaitskell, who neatly turned the tables on everybody. 'I am shocked by the stance of everybody who has spoken so far ... in thinking and speaking of sex, physical sex, as something dirty, something animal in the pejorative sense,' she said, and went on to say of Longford *et al.*, 'Nor do I regard shockability as a test of virtue. People are prone to be more easily shocked as they grow older, as we see here today.'

What of the evidence? Everybody mentioned Denmark but nobody had the facts. In any case, it was generally agreed that what facts there were should be dismissed.

> Some very sincere people have proven to their own satisfaction that there are no deleterious consequences of all this. There was an extraordinary United States Congressional Commission on obscenity and pornography and they came to something of that conclusion. I was not surprised that their recommendations were thrown out (Lord Beswick).

Why was he not surprised? Lord Eccles, the first Minister for the Arts to consider actually issuing a poetic licence, explained:

> The belief that some thoughts can poison the mind and corrupt the character has been central to the teaching of the world's greatest religions and philosophies. Can it really make sense to throw away the wisdom of the ages just because modern science can show us more clearly the causes of sexual deviations and of the urge to violence?

Well, no, since you put it like that, we suppose not. Regrettably, the wisdom of the ages is not always the same as the wisdom of the aged. And like Stork and Butter, sometimes it's difficult to tell what you're being offered.

In a debate chiefly notable for its assumptions, there were a few good arguments. 'Are we talking about highly commercialised sex?' asked Baroness Lee of Asheridge,

> It is a bore ... perhaps what we are trying to do in this debate is not so much to change things as to get some of the dirt out of sight ... there is something to be said for that. I am all in favour of good sanitation. But I do not think we should pretend this afternoon that we are doing very much more than that.

Baroness Gaitskell described how 'the communications explosion has thrown a grenade into our ideas of morality' and got nearer the heart of the question than most. Lord Ardwick made a good point:

> Vast numbers of people seem to need constant reassurance that sexual feelings are not sinful feelings. That is why ... there is such a large market for newspaper and magazine articles that claim ... to deal frankly with sexual problems. The fact that many of these articles are tedious and repetitious does nothing to detract from them. It is not information which the readers are primarily seeking; it is simply reassurance.

And from the other side, several of the old Longfordians made out a case against pornography while ignoring the separate if complementary question of whether or not what is bad should automatically be banned.

Repetition pays off. The customer is captured if he sees or hears over and over again that Guinness or a pint of milk is good for him. Why should it be any different if he sees and hears over and over again that sex has nothing to do with love and that violence is a normal way of getting what you want? (Lord Eccles).

'I think that basically pornography is simply another form of atmospheric pollution, neither more nor less' (Viscount Norwich).

The debate had no conclusion. As a postscript, the last paragraph of Lord Strange's speech had little to say about pornography, but, we feel, becomes highly relevant if we apply it to Lord Longford and the debate itself:

The last thing I would say is that I was in the Windward Isles on a banana boat and I got to know where all the floozy pubs were and I got to know the lounge lizards. I asked a taxi driver to take me to a 'toughish joint' to see what the natives were like. I had some beer and I talked to a few people. I saw on the wall a notice and I have it here written on the matchbox on which I wrote it then. It said: 'Lord help us against ourselves.'

JOYNSON HICKS WILLIAM (1865–1939): Viscount Brentford; statesman; educated at Merchant Taylor's School; admitted solicitor, 1887, Conservative M.P. North-West Manchester (1908–10), Brentford (1911–18), Twickenham (1918–29), especially interested in road traffic and aviation, Home Secretary 1924–9; dealt successfully with general strike 1926, President National Church League 1921, prominent in defeat of prayer book revision 1927–8.

After his anti-alien campaign, Jix (Joynson Hicks) moved towards his second objective, sex. Sex was a beastly invention which was fast turning London into a sewer, but he would destroy it. The police agreed with Jix. They assured the Home Secretary of their utmost loyalty to his mission. They would not flinch from helping him mop up all the sex in London, even if it meant their coming into contact with the beastly thing. Jix was troubled that such a decent, clean-limbed body of men should have to concern itself with such an unspeakable task and as a reward he promised the police an affection and loyalty such as no Home Secretary had shown the Force in all its existence ... The police raided the Warren Gallery where D. H. Lawrence's painting were on view. 'Stephen', the heroine of *The Well,* as it was called, went to court like *Lady Chatterley* and was defended by a great many distinguished people. But all to no purpose. *The Well* was tucked away with other porn behind a screen of Sappers and Dornford Yateses in the Charing Cross Road. Quite a few prosecutions of this nature occurred, though when the police seized the drawings of William Blake it was almost too much and indignation was drowned in laughter ... Jix's policy had a great effect on the Lord Chamberlain, though Jix emphatically denied that he was against the theatre. It was true, he said, that he was against 'problem plays'. But no one enjoyed an evening's entertainment by Mr Tom Walls and Mr Ralph Lynn more than he. – compiled from the *Dictionary of National Biography,* and *The Age of Illusion* by Ronald Blythe.

JUDGES: SPECIAL OZ JUDGES ISSUE: Edited by Justice Dribble, 107: Justice Ongatwilight, 69; Justice Goddard (dec'd as a direct result of this opus) and many other eminent men who wish to remain anonymous for the sake of their children.

SAVE THE ARGYLE says Sir Herbert Farquing, QC, AC, DC ... Unless stern measures are taken the forces of oppression may render this species extinct. The Argyle who has been with us longer than human memory is threatened by pollution, drugs and unsolicited obscene males dropping in through his letter box.

OLD JOKE. He is a symbol of all we hold most often. A raconteur, he is often to be seen in the club, swopping risqué yarns with his brethren from the bar.

ALTERNATIVE SOCIETY. He represents for many a new and exciting life-style. His unconventional apparel and nylon wig have been mocked and derided, but what could be more open and human and natural than to 'drag up' from time to time, and to feign deafness when confronted by such notorious bores as Farty Meldman and Richard Neville Chamberlain waving his little bit of paper.

ACTION. The staff of OZ*zz*zzz say the time has come to take to the streets and show their supports. A mass sleep-in, led by Sir Cyril Black and Mary Whitehouse will be held at The Sleezirama non-stop nudibar as a counter measure to the tide of smut, drugs and obscenity which we are constantly forced to buy. JOIN US if you can get out of bed and wave your Daily Telegraph.

BECK SHOCK. Justice Spruling Beck was found guilty by Germaine Greer of driving a wheel chair, whilst under the influence of Madeira. He was summarily castrated and bound over for a period of 12 months. Miss Greer, 73, in passing sentence said: 'I have one a month. Why shouldn't he have one for a year.' His Worship said later: 'I shall be appealing to the House of Lords and, if necessary, to Dorothy Squires.'

HARD CORE – Reg Throbb, describing himself as a full-time Soho pornographer was found guilty of not attempting to bribe the police at Bow Street yesterday. Defending himself, Throbb, 43, 43, 43, said: 'I can't afford it. All my regulars have switched to Vivian Neves in The Times.'

KNACKERS LIBRARY RAIDED. The offices of Inspector 'Knackers of the Yard' Knackers were busted last night by a group of wild-eyed middle-aged men who seized a quantity of allegedly obscene material. Inspector Knackers, speaking from his hospital bed said: 'I suspect the Vatican.'

JUDGES TREATED LIKE DOGS by Lunchtime O'Qceeze ... Temple Bar, Thursday. Desperate judges were selling their bodies and those of their wives in a degrading attempt to secure appointments for obscenity trials. Their craving for publicity has reduced them to shambling wrecks. I saw, with my own eyes, one of these pathetic long-haired victims kneel and beg for a fix. 'I know I'm addicted,' he gasped, his bloodshot eyes rolling violently. 'Once you're on the obscenity trip, you can't get off. I wish I had stuck to driving offences but it's too late. I'm on the hard stuff now.'

SMALL ADS: *Elderly Judge*—Docile, seeks dominant QC. Must share interests in leatherwear and discipline. Photo appreciated. *Virile Silk* interested photography and mixed sauna, seeks qualified masseur/masseurs. View marriage. *Recently Deceased* judge interested in meeting necrophiliacs with view to prosecuting them posthumously. *Naomi ... Bring Back the Cat: I Can't Get To Sleep Without Him!!!!' We Can Use* —your old black stockings, wigs and frilly underwear. Send anything you've got to *Judgefam*.

SMALL LADS. *Retired Judge* seeks lively youngster for manual labour. No qualifications required but must be willing to submit to an oral. Photos appreciated and certainly not sent back. *Juvenile Delinquent* needed to join lively discussion group. GBH refs. essential. *If You Are* a young boy who needs teaching a lesson why not pop down to the Inns of Court for a spanking good time.

PERSONAL. *Minor Sex Problems* can often be overcome by hanging. Money back guarantee if no ejaculation. *Unretouched Pics* of Justice Melford Stevens in conventional poses. Hurry! Hurry! Hurry! while stocks last. *Stocks Wanted.* Also whips, canes, racks, thumbscrews and any other instruments of justice.

From *Private Eye*, 1971.

LADY CHATTERLEY'S LOVER: D. H. Lawrence's novel was banned in anything but an expurgated edition from its first appearance in 1928, to the good lady's reprieve by jury in 1960, when she was acquitted, along with Penguin books, of her reputed tendencies to deprave and corrupt, 2,000,000 people then bought the 3/6 full edition and Christopher Booker argued in *his* book *The Neophiliacs,* that liberal intellectual enthusiasts had gone potty. He quoted Juvenal: 'High flown moral discourse from that clique in Rome, who affect ancestral peasant virtues as a front for their lechery.' Be that as it may, and in fact it may not, we quote suitable extracts from her trial, remembering that the Prosecution's attack withered in front of defence Counsel's 35 expert witnesses, changed in vain to assaulting her position as an adulteress, then hinted too late of buggery during 'the night of sensual passion'. Her vindication cost Penguin Books £13,000 (in return for some good publicity) from a Judge who refused to allow the case to be paid for from public funds although it was acknowledged as a test case.

Mr Griffith-Jones (in his opening address for the Prosecution):

You may think that one of the ways in which you can test this book, and test it from the most liberal outlook, is to ask yourself the question, when you have read it through, would you approve of your young sons, young daughters—because girls can read as well as boys—reading this book. Is it a book that you would have lying around in your own house? Is it a book that you would even wish your wife or your servants to read? ... Lady Chatterley is a young woman whose husband was wounded in the First World War. They were married at the beginning of the war; he comes back wounded so that he is crippled and paralysed from the waist downwards and unable to have any sexual intercourse. Members of the jury, other views may be put before you; I invite you to say that, in effect, the book is a book describing how that woman, deprived of sex from her husband, satisfies her sexual desires—a sex-starved girl—how she satisfies that starvation with a particularly sensual man who happens to be her husband's gamekeeper.

The only variations, in effect, between all thirteen occasions are the time and the *locus in quo*, the place where it happened. So one does not follow them into the bed and remain with them in bed; one starts in my lady's boudoir, in her husband's house, one goes to the floor of a hut in the forest with a blanket laid down as a bed; we see them do it again in the undergrowth in the forest amongst the shrubbery, and not only in the undergrowth in the forest, in the pouring rain, both of them stark naked and dripping with raindrops.

The book abounds in bawdy conversation. Even a description of the girl's father, a Royal Academician, has to introduce a description of his legs and loins; and, members of the Jury, even the old nurse who is eventually employed to look after her husband, the heroine's husband, without any point to it whatsoever, without adding anything at all, you may think, to the story, has to have her breasts felt while she is looking after him in bed.

These matters are not voiced normally in this Court, but when it forms the whole subject matter of the Prosecution, then, members of the Jury, we cannot avoid voicing them. The word 'fuck' or 'fucking' occurs no less than thirty times. I have added them up, but I do not guarantee that I have added them all up. 'Cunt' fourteen times; 'balls' thirteen times; 'shit' and 'arse' six times apiece; 'cock' four times; 'piss' three times, and so on ...

Members of the Jury, for those of you who have forgotten your Greek, 'phallus' means the image of the man's penis ...

What is your view as to the genuineness and necessity of this book of the use of these four-letter words in the mouth of Mellors?

Richard Hoggart: They seem to be totally characteristic of many people, and I would like to say not only working-class people, because that would be wrong. They are used, or seem to me to be used, very freely indeed, far more freely than many of us know. Fifty yards from this Court this morning I heard a man say 'fuck' three times as he passed me. He was speaking to himself and he said 'fuck it, fuck it, fuck it' as he went by.

G-J: What about tenderness? Is that a theme which it is in the public good to read as expressed in this book? I will tell you how it is expressed in this book, in the words of the book itself 'Tenderness, really cunt tenderness. Sex is really the closest touch of all. Cunt tenderness.' That is the tenderness that this book is advocating through the mouth of one of its chief characters.

'And not only was he committing adultery, but he was committing adultery with somebody else who was committing adultery ...'

'Connie went slowly home ... Another self was alive in her, burning molten and soft in her womb and bowels, and with this self she adored him ...'

I suppose that is good writing, or is that ludicrous?

R. H.: Not to me.

G-J: 'In her womb and bowels'—again we have got the same two parts of her anatomy coupled together within three lines. 'She was flowing and alive now ...' I do not want to be unimaginative, believe me, but can one flow and be alive in one's womb and bowels?

R. H.: Metaphorically, I think one can.

G-J: Even metaphorically?

R. H.: Yes.

We leave Court with Prosecuting Counsel producing the finest *double-entente* of the whole trial:

'It was a night of sensual passion, in which she was a little startled and almost unwilling: yet it pierced again with piercing thrills of sensuality, different, sharper, more terrible than the thrills of tenderness, but, at the moment, more desirable. Though a little frightened, she let him have his way...'

Not very easy sometimes, sometimes, not very easy, you know, to know what in fact he is driving at *in that passage*. (Our italics.)

LAWRENCE: D. H., writer and author of *The Rainbow, Women In Love, Lady Chatterley's Lover* etc., had his life and work plagued by the censors. His ghost is equally strenuously fought over. Both the permissive and the reactionary lobby have claimed him for their own, and both have a point. Lawrence wrote several essays on the subject of obscenity and pornography. But he wrote about them as an artist, not as a moralist or a lawyer. Indeed he shared with Dickens and a long chain of English writers an almost physical distaste for the law. 'The law is a dreary thing and its judgements have nothing to do with life,' he wrote, and he described a clerk who served a bankruptcy order on him as a 'grubby creature'.

No, his views on sex materials are probably the ones we would most of us take, ideally. He dismissed

> the idea that sex appeal in art is pornography. It may be so to the grey Puritan, but the grey Puritan is a sick man, body and soul sick, so why should we bother about his hallucinations?

Yet, he attacked 'the attempt to insult sex, to do dirt on it. That is unpardonable.' He was a bitter opponent of the dirty postcard, the smoking-room story, the pornographic book. But he believed that all these attempts 'to do dirt on sex' existed only because of the repression of true sexual feelings. 'Without secrecy there would be no pornography.' And the greatest 'dirty little secret' of all was sex itself.

Lawrence wrote at a time when the sexual revolution among the young was a current *idea,* but before it had struggled into practice. He gave the young full credit for their ideas.

> Personally, among themselves, a great many, perhaps a majority of the young people of today have come out into the open with sex and laid salt on the tail of the dirty little secret. But in public, in the social world, the young are still entirely under the shadow of the grey elderly ones.

And Lawrence, naturally, was not able to see what would happen when they ceased to be under that shadow, or began to emerge from it. Some things he foresaw. He worried, for example,

> the danger is that, in killing the dirty little secret, you will kill dynamic sex altogether and leave only the scientific and deliberate mechanism.

His reservations about the sex educators like Marie Stopes could be shared, in some measure, by Muggeridge or Whitehouse. But he could not foresee everything.

Lawrence is an amazingly good guide to what is absolutely and finally true about obscenity and pornography (and incidentally, he surely said the last word on definitions: 'What they are depends, as usual, entirely on the individual'). He is a less accurate guide to what is relatively, and—in a given society—should be, done and thought about them. No one can say what Lawrence would have made of our own society, where, briefly, sex has come out into the open but where the midwife of its revolution has been great and unprecedented commercial pressures and where 'the grey ones' still sit, however uncomfortably, in the seats of power. And most of society occupies an undignified position in between freedom and repression: a kind of prurient hypocrisy. There is not that much difference between *On the Buses* and the smoking-room stories Lawrence so detested.

Thus Lawrence can say he would 'censor genuine pornography, rigorously', but he was never in a position where he had to think about that statement. He was still fighting to get *The Rainbow* cleared and the judicial approval for *Lady Chatterley* was 30 years away. Since his time, far more has been researched and written and even scientifically investigated about the content and effects of hard-core porn. And at the same time the threats to the individual freedom Lawrence prized so much have multiplied to a point where pornography scarcely seems the most dangerous or the most promising. And we have far more experience, too, of what censorship means. Censor genuine pornography rigorously? We might be in favour if it didn't mean throwing out the baby with the bathwater, *Lady Chatterley* with *Men Only*—while *Playboy* would still sneak through the legal net. The law and morals, tempting though they may be for a one-night stand, don't marry. The evils of a censorship which, in the true moral sense Lawrence fought for so brilliantly, isn't effective anyway, outweigh the evils of a freedom which, who knows, one day might be.

We can't leave Lawrence without pointing out that some of his writing on sex and sex materials is wrong. He was an artist. What is a philosophy to Norman Mailer—'only connect'—was for him an instinctive way of working. But the connexions that in fiction could carry him past reason into insight, in law or morals or politics could carry him past reason into a truth which is neither useful nor wholly true. He said of masturbation

> When the grey ones wail that the young man and the young woman went and had sexual intercourse they are bewailing the fact that the young man and the young woman didn't go separately and masturbate. Sex must go somewhere, especially in young people. So in our glorious civilization it goes in masturbation ... is masturbation so harmless though? Is it even comparatively pure and harmless? Not to my thinking ... the great danger of masturbation lies in its purely exhaustive nature. In sexual intercourse

> there is give and take ... but in masturbation there is nothing but loss ... The real masturbation of Englishmen began only in the nineteenth century. It has continued with an increasing emptying of the real vitality and the real being of men till now people are little more than shells of people.

This is masturbation not so much as personal practice but as social and political myth. It is, like Lawrence's view of the history of painting since the Renaissance, bound up with the fear of venereal disease. 'Never trust the artist, trust the tale,' Lawrence also said, and went on: 'The proper function of the critic is to save the tale from the artist who created it.' But artists have a fund of low cunning. And the most cunning trick of all is to dress your tale up as a statement of fact, naked, innocent non-fiction, as Lawrence does in his essays.

One final irony: every sex book publisher and magazine editor and nude photographer we talked to described 1960 and the *Lady Chatterley* Trial as the turning point in the spread of 'obscenity and pornography' in Britain. How Lawrence would have hated that? Oh, surely. But also, and certainly, how he would have laughed! (see also *Lady Chatterley's Lover* and *Erotic Art*).

LONGFORD: FRANCIS AUNGIER (origin of the expression 'Aungier than thou') **PAKENHAM**, seventh Earl. Born, December 5, 1905. Patrician, scholar, Labour and Catholic convert, politician, writer, autobiographer, amateur missionary.

Addresses: 18, Chesil Court, Chelsea Manor Street, London SW3. Telephone: 01-352-7794. Bernhurst, Hurst Green, Sussex. Telephone: Hurst Green 248.

His father, the fifth Earl (the sixth Earl was Francis Pakenham's elder brother) was an Irish landlord and at one time master of the Westmeath Hounds. He was His Majesty's Lieutenant for the County of Longford. The family owed its estates to the gratitude of Oliver Cromwell for services rendered by one of their ancestors. In 1915 he was killed in the Dardanelles. According to contemporary accounts of his death:

> Longford knew where he wanted to get to and walked straight there at the head of his brigade, under a very heavy fire with his

> walking stick in his hand ... Longford was right in front all the time and only stopped to light his pipe ... Poor Longford knew where he wanted to get to and went for it bald-headed and got there ...

According to a later account: he 'was supposed to be the bravest man in the British Army. He was a magnificent figure in his cuirass, just like a Viking.' Lord Longford says of his father's death that it 'has always represented for me the one unassailable image of conduct at once glorious and pure.' The Brigadier was 50 at the time of his death. Francis was nine.

1918: Eton. Among his contemporaries and near contemporaries were Sir Alec Douglas-Home; Lord Hailsham; Duncan Sandys; Cyril Connolly; George Orwell. Many of the young Francis's schoolmates were destined later in their lives to sit in the House of Lords. Of boys passing through Eton at this time (born between 1900 and 1910), the following were peers in 1971: Abercorn, Ailesbury, Allenby, Allerton, Ancaster, Arran, Ashton of Hyde, Baldwin, Bearsted, Beauchamp, Beaufort, Birkenhead, Boothby, Braye, Camrose, Chilston, Churston, Clitheroe, Cobbold, Cobham, Colyton, Cottesloe, Courtown, the Bishop of Coventry, Lords Cowdray, Craigavon, Cranbrook, Crawford and Balcarres, Daresbury, Daryngton, de Clifford, Delamere, De la Warr, De l'Isle and Dudley, Denman, Dilhorne (the former Sir Reginald Manningham-Buller), Donaldson, Donegall, Drogheda, Essex, Exeter, Falkland, Faringdon, Fitzwilliam, Forteviot, Gladwyn, Glasgow, Gore-Booth, Goschen, Grenfell, Gretton, Hailsham (the former Quintin Hogg), Halsbury, Hamilton, Hampden, Harcourt, Hardwicke, Harmsworth, Hazelrigg, Head, Hood, Howe, Huntingdon, Jersey, Jessel, Kensington, Kilmany, Leicester, Leigh, Luke, Lurgan, Malmesbury, Margadale, Mersey, Merthyr, Monck, Monsell, Montrose, Moyne, Nunburnholme, Oranmore and Browne, Penrhyn, Poulett, Powerscourt, Rayleigh, Redcliffe-Maud, Reigate, Renwick, Rhyl (the former Nigel Birch), Richmond and Gordon, Rochdale, Rockley, Rothes, Runciman, Selkirk, Stair, Stonehaven, Strange, Swinfen, Thorneycroft (the former Peter Thorneycroft), Thurlow, Tollemache, Tryon, Upjohn, Vivian, Ward, Westminster, and Wolverton. Of these only three became Labour peers. Only one, Pakenham, became a practising Labour politician.

Francis was an active sportsman but did not qualify as a member of the exclusive Eton society, Pop. When he thought of applying for election, a friend took him aside and said: 'I think you ought to know that you are the most unpopular boy in the school.'

1924: New College, Oxford. His close friends now included Lord Birkenhead, David Cecil, Evelyn Waugh, Aidan Crawley, Peter Fleming, and two Socialists: Hugh Gaitskell and Evan Durbin. Later his Socialist friends included Richard Crossman and Patrick Gordon Walker: the three of them played together in the same Rugby XV. Took one of the best two firsts in his year in Modern Greats at Oxford.

Francis Pakenham made a fetish of fitness, running around Christ Church Meadow twice a day, three times when he felt inspired.

In 1928, having taken his degree, he was still in Oxford, reading law. He took part in a point-to-point race organised by the Bullingdon Club: among other competitors were Aidan Crawley and William, later Lord, Astor. His horse fell at the first fence. He remounted and chased after the field, only to fall again, badly, at the end of the first circuit. Consoling friends set him back on his horse, brushed him down, and urged him to resume. A few minutes later, he saw William Astor coming at him, riding in the opposite direction. Pausing only to point out to Astor that he was riding the wrong way round the course—and unmoved by Astor's insistence that it was he, Pakenham, who was at fault—he went bald-headed for the line and got there, only to find that it was the starting line; he had completed the course in reverse.

1929: worked briefly on the Stock Exchange. Then combined two jobs: member of the Conservative Research Department; and teacher and workers' education tutor at Audley near Stoke, Staffordshire.

> As a boy in Oxfordshire and in Westmeath, and later on at the Eton Manor Boys' Club, I had mixed a good deal with working men and boys. I had always been attracted by their special qualities. But up till that time I had never really lived among them. (Lord Pakenham, *Born to Believe*, Jonathan Cape, 1953, p. 60).

After a time, Pakenham began to notice a curious incompatibility between the doctrines promulgated from the Conservative Research

Department and the living conditions of the Potteries in the early thirties. For the moment, however, he remained a Conservative.

1931: married Elizabeth, daughter of Nathaniel Harman, ophthalmic surgeon. Elizabeth Harman was a friend of Hugh Gaitskell's. In an interview with the *Daily Mail* in February, 1972, she said:

> He was asleep, alone in a chair in the middle of a midsummer ball. I stopped, gazed at the sleeping prince and wondered: How could some fool of a girl have let him out of her clutches? He was so super, so wonderful, so dazzlingly good looking. He had a mass of untidy, curly hair—it would have looked quite natural these days. I was reading classics and to me he looked like a Graeco-Roman statue, except that he had nice pink cheeks. The following day, after another ball, I saw the same handsome figure asleep on a couch, in my friend Hugh Gaitskell's room. I couldn't swear to it, but he says that I woke him with a kiss. It was tremendously romantic. Like the *Sleeping Beauty* in reverse.

1932: after an unsuccessful spell as a leader writer on the *Daily Mail*, Pakenham became a lecturer, later student, in politics at Christ Church, Oxford.

1935: converted to Socialism. (His wife had been a Socialist since her first acquaintance with economic conditions in the Potteries.) 'I had come to believe that the Labour party was far more interested than any other party in human equality and far more likely therefore to promote social and international justice.' (*Born to Believe*, p. 243). The final decision came after he had seen and suffered violence at a Mosley meeting in Oxford.

1937: Oxford City Councillor. Secretary of Oxford City Labour party; briefly a parliamentary candidate in Birmingham, where he bought a Labour weekly, the *Town Crier*, installing Philip Toynbee as editor. Later became Labour candidate for Oxford City.

1939: joined the 5th (Territorial) Battalion of the Oxford and Bucks Light Infantry. ('When I marched down the High Street at the rear of our column there was much tittering and pointing from bystanders.')

When war began 'it was conveyed to me that an application for a commission might be acceptable.' Promoted 2nd lieutenant. (John Sparrow, now warden of All Souls, was one of his lance corporals.) Invalided out, 1940, after repeated attacks of gastric flu 'got to work on a nervous system already strained'. Always mindful of his father's bravery in the 1914–18 war, he felt deeply 'the pain of my civilian status ... The wound will never, I suppose, heal completely.'

Commanded South company, Oxford City Batallion, Home Guard, with Maurice Bowra as Second-in-Command. Sustained a war wound when a college cook, who was being given instruction in how to use a gun, accidentally shot him in the foot.

1940: received into the Roman Catholic Church, shortly before being invalided out of the Army.

> I never doubted, and by the grace of God, have never doubted since, that I had taken the right step, or that the Catholic Church provided that peace and ultimate security which had so tragically escaped the world outside, and must continue to escape them so long as they depended on themselves. (ibid, p. 117).

1941: assistant to Lord Beveridge on his Report and in subsequent research. 1945: *Fought Oxford City for Labour,* but was defeated by Quintin Hogg. Many of his friends won seats elsewhere. On the day of the declaration of his result, Evan Durbin, one of the brightest of the young Labour entrants, arrived from Edmonton, having won his seat. 'We must get you into Parliament somehow,' was the burden of Evan's message. 'If not into one House, then into the other.' Pakenham was then taken to see Hugh Dalton, who was staying at Burford.

> He visualised my position with alacrity, insisted that I must at all costs be associated with the great social experiment that was about to be conducted, and that evening found time to write letters to about half a dozen leading members of the Government, commending me to their notice. (ibid. p. 152).

Became personal assistant to Arthur Greenwood, Lord Privy Seal *Accepted Attlee's invitation to sit as a Labour peer,* becoming Lord Pakenham of Cowley, with a government appointment as Lord in Waiting (a government whip). He was 39—the youngest peer to be awarded a title since Beaverbrook in 1916.

1946: *Under-secretary for War.* 1947: Chancellor of the Duchy of Lancaster, with responsibility for the British zones of Germany and Austria.

> Christians have had less excuse than others for ignoring the cal

to forgive the German people and to join in their immense task of redemption. (ibid, p. 246).

On a tour of Dusseldorf, then in the midst of 'an appalling food crisis' he was taken to a school housed in an air raid shelter and asked whether he would like to hear the children sing. He asked that they should sing the *Miserere*:

> Wash me thoroughly from my wickedness; and cleanse me from my sin. For I acknowledge my faults; and my sin is ever before me ... Behold, I was shapen in wickedness; and in sin hath my mother conceived me. But lo, thou requirest truth in the inward parts; and shalt make me to understand wisdom secretly. Thou shalt purge me with hyssop, and I shall be clean: thou shalt wash me, and I shall be whiter than snow ... The sacrifice of God is a troubled spirit: a broken and contrite heart, O God shalt thou not despise ...

'While the children were repeating it very reverentially, one of them fainted, an obviously unrehearsed, but remarkably dramatic effect.' (*Born to Believe,* p. 176).

Pakenham became identified as a champion of German interests, to the annoyance of Ernest Bevin, who thought he was too sentimental. He contemplated resigning, but in 1948 *was transferred to become Minister of Civil Aviation.*

In May 1951, appointed First Lord of the Admiralty; but five months later, Labour was defeated in a general election.

1952–64: *Returned to Christ Church,* teaching politics. *1955–63*: *Chairman, National Bank*. *1964*: *Lord Privy Seal and Leader of the House of Lords* in the new Labour Government: *Secretary of State for the Colonies, 1965–6*; *Lord Privy Seal again thereafter,* continuing to lead the Lords. *Resigned, January 1969,* in protest against the Government's refusal to stand by its decision to raise the school-leaving age.

Lord Longford as author: In 1953, published his autobiography, *Born to Believe.* (He was then 48.) In 1964, he followed this with another autobiographical work, *Five Lives* (Hutchinson). In this book he expresses dissatisfaction with *Born to Believe*. In 1969, he published *Humility* (Collins, Fontana Books), a book with a strong auto-biographical tendency, in the course of which he expresses dissatisfaction with both *Born to Believe* and *Five Lives.* Other works include a biography (with Thomas O'Neill) of De Valera; *Peace by Ordeal* (a study of the Anglo-Irish treaty of 1921); *Causes of Crime* (with Roger Opie: based on a study he carried out for the Nuffield Foundation but which the Foundation did not publish); and *The Idea of Punishment. Since 1970 he has been chairman of the publishing house of Sidgwick and Jackson.*

Lord Longford as family man: the Longfords have four sons and three daughters: a fourth daughter was killed in a road accident. The book *Five Lives* ends with a portrait of 'The author as a father' by his daughter Judith, which describes Lord Longford

> on his knees beside the drawing room sofa saying his good-night prayers before he goes to bed ... a little comic, so large on the floor, not sitting up like any civilised man on the sofa, it has always seemed characteristic of my father's gentle persistent effort to do as he thought right, however uncomfortable it might look to others.

Lord Longford as missionary. 'To hate the sin and love the sinner is the kernel of wisdom.' (*Humility* p. 127). 'We are all miserable sinners but all infinitely dear to God, all of us lying in the gutter with our eyes fixed on the stars.' (ibid).

Lord Longford visits a doss house, November 1962. Capt. Noel Lister-Binns, 34-year-old head of a group of voluntary social workers, went with him. 'Lord Longford's manner was just so easy,' he says. 'He just sat himself down in these places next to someone and said: "My name's Frank Longford," and asked the man questions about himself.'

Saving young ladies from sin, December 1967. The story of a peer who helped a prostitute has been told in the magazine *Christian Action.* 'I had no serious hopes that a talk with me would persuade her to leave her back street haunts,' he said. (But it did: after conversations with Lord Longford, she had foresworn prostitution and was now in a convent, contemplating nunhood.) Sunday newspaper report.

Peter Wildeblood. (Wildeblood, with Lord Montagu, was jailed for 18 months for homosexual offences.)

> Two things kept me going. One was the visit, every three weeks, of Lord Pakenham. Sitting with him there in a room without a warder, in the dingy grey suit which I had worn for six months, with my hands scarred by the mailbag needle and my

fingernails black with ingrained dirt, I could feel that I was still a person. I can never repay him for what he did for me during those months ... *Against the Law* (*Penguin, 1955*).

Among other celebrated prisoners he has visited: Christopher Craig, jailed for his part in a murder on a Croydon roof top in 1952 (his companion Derek Bentley was executed). Michael Davies, sentenced to death for a murder on Clapham Common in 1953 but reprieved. The Moors Murderers, Ian Brady and Myra Hindley. Lord Longford has made countless speeches both in and out of Parliament in the cause of prison reform.

He founded 'The New Bridge,' a society to help ex-prisoners, and has also been involved in work for drug addicts in London. His sympathies extend to other minorities in need of help. As the *Daily Herald* reported in March 1963:

When Lord Longford meets an African in the tube on his way to work, he always makes a point of saying 'good morning'.

Lord Longford explained to the peers last night that he did this to promote racial harmony. He confessed that African men were sometimes puzzled by his greeting—'and if the African is a lady it sometimes leads to misunderstandings'.

But he intends to persist in his attempt to show friendship to Africans.

Lord Longford and the Permissive Society. In the *Sunday Times* of November 7, 1971, Lord Longford wrote:

For myself I am neither for nor against the so-called permissive society. In so far as it represents a more compassionate attitude towards outcasts—prisoners, drug addicts, unmarried mothers—I am utterly for it. And just as utterly against it if it offers an invitation to promiscuity in sex and self-indulgence generally. What really matters is whether we are a caring society or a non-caring society. A caring society is one which loves the sinner but hates the sin and, still more fundamentally, is determined to eradicate the causes of sin and to heal the sickness of the mind.

In a Lords debate on the Wolfenden Report, Lord Longford said he believed that, by and large, they could accept the view of the committee on whether the law should intervene where a man was doing wrong with another person. He did not say it would be morally wrong in all cases for the State to intervene to save people from themselves. If there was to be interference the onus was on the Government to justify it by exceptional conditions.

On the two other important social reform issues of the late 1960s, however, he took – as might have been expected from a senior Catholic politician – a hostile view. *On abortion law reform,* he said in the House of Lords that he was

> horrified, indeed terrified, by what might lie behind it. If we pass these measures, we are driving in the thin end of a wedge whose final limit may well be foreseen by the promoters of this Bill, but I would guess by few others, perhaps by hardly anyone in this House ... the execution time of old people may not be so very far off.

The Divorce Bill, he told the Lords, contained certain essential features which were 'utterly evil'.

Like most missionaries, Lord Longford has always found it hard (whatever the principles he might have expressed as an official party spokesman of the Wolfenden Report) to stand idly by and let people set their own standards of behaviour.

The natives must be made to wear Mother Hubbards, whether they wish it or not.

When he asserts that we are all lying in the gutter with our eyes fixed on the stars, it is no use our replying, 'Speak for yourself'. Lord Longford knows better than we do where we are lying and on what our eyes are fixed. 'Poor Longford knew where he wanted to get to and went for it bald-headed ...' 'The immense task of redemption ...' 'However uncomfortable it may look to others ...'

> In the history books, the man of political courage is the man who stands alone against the crowd or who braves what Dr Johnson would have called the hiss of the world. In the words of the hymn my brother used to sing so often:
>
> Dare to be a Daniel
> Dare to stand alone
> Dare to have a purpose true
> And dare to make it known.
>
> (*Humility*, page 28).

And remember that there is no possibility, no possibility at all, that you may be riding the wrong way round the course.

MAGAZINES: The magazines under scrutiny by those who are concerned about pornography are, broadly speaking, of three types: hard-core pornography, easily identifiable because it consists very simply of photographs of sexual activities (pornography by anyone's definition, though not necessarily harmful by the same precepts), soft-core pornography, which is still basically concerned with the graphic representation of sexual activity, and the relatively recent phenomenon of sex magazines, considered by many to be part of the soft-core business. It is the blurred lines drawn between these last two groups that cause most confusion and concern. We can more or less dismiss hard-core from this discussion since they are hardly magazines in any real sense of the word. They rarely have any text, are usually concerned with detailed depictions of fetishist sexual activity (often sado-masochistic), often don't get beyond the first number and are interchangeable with any other magazine of the same type. They are, in fact, booklets printed in magazine format and by magazine processes. They are usually from abroad and sell at £2–£10. A slim magazine bought in Denmark for 50p will cost about £7 in Soho. Some of these 'magazines', though not the most expensive variety, can be returned to the shop after use at a 50 per cent discount on a further purchase. This encourages regulars and the Soho trade depends on its regular customers. This hard-core material is referred to as 'books' rather than 'magazines' by the trade, and even though the use of the word is not uncommon for magazines in all fields, in pornography it is quite specific and acknowledges that they aren't monthly publications that are supposed to go on for ever. And they aren't on open sale. Magazines, like most products in pornography, are marketed mainly by the entrepreneurs who cash in on every semi-legal fad. Soft-core porn mags are almost without exception badly written, badly designed and badly produced. This is because the mechanics of pornography (at least in its widely-accepted usage) revolve around profit maximisation—in other words, minimal expenditure for maximal returns.

Printing in this country is more expensive than in Scandinavia or the States, which is one reason why there is not yet here the proliferation of full-colour magazines to be seen in those two places. Magazines over here cost 40 or 50 pence, a price that may be prohibitive for the merely curious reader but one that is quite acceptable to the porn punter; this is fortunate for the pornmonger since a full-colour magazine, even if economically produced, has to sell anything up to 20,000 copies to make a profit. Simple black-and-white magazines (these are usually the small-format variety) are much cheaper and only need to sell 5,000 or so to break even. A well-produced colour magazine, with articles and photographs commissioned and paid for at usual journalistic rates, costs at least £5,000 an edition to produce and print.

The distributors of 'semi-porn' (and a national distributor is vital if the magazine is to sell the required 20,000) can demand a much higher percentage because of the 'risk' involved, although the distributors are rarely, if ever, implicated in any obscenity charges. The distributor is usually the one link in the chain that can't lose, since editor, publisher, printer and retailer are all often involved in any subsequent legal action.

The normal business strategies of magazines are rarely applied to soft-core porn although they may well become big business: the objective is inevitably short-term profitability and, in the jargon of marketing, they have a 'finite time horizon'—probably only a couple of years—so that there is little point in the publisher creating any 'brand loyalty' or in slowly building up a regular readership from a selected socio-economic class. He isn't interested in taking advertising (or, more correctly, advertisers aren't interested in the sex market) so his revenue is solely from sales.

Apart from these easily-available soft-core magazines (at the latest count, getting on for a score as opposed to a mere two a year previously) there is the harder material, that still doesn't quite qualify as hard-core, available in selected areas. These retail outlets are generally Soho-type bookshops or so-called sex supermarkets (see *Anne Summers*), but other specialised spots also exist: for example in a chain of cinema clubs a range of magazines is on sale ranging from semi-respectable sex mags to others that look as if they might originate in the USA—that is, from medium to hot. Certain soft-core magazines advertise harder-core magazines. Quite often the same distributor handles the whole temperature range.

These latter magazines have always been a feature of the sort of market typified by the Soho grey-raincoat brigade. The only difference in the past few years has been the increase in numbers, the more open display in shop windows and the drop in price (for example, while a few years ago a typical American soft-penis porn mag—one that shows genitalia but not actual intercourse—would cost £5 or so, this sort of magazine now only costs a couple of pounds and a British equivalent sells at just over £1). The market has probably expanded, but the sale is still confined more or less to shops where the client knows exactly what he is about and where an unwary innocent is unlikely to wander in and be surprised and offended. For this reason they are considered less of a public nuisance than more openly-available soft-core magazines, although there is the occasional raid to remind the porn merchants (most of Soho is actually in the hands of the Maltese) that the police shouldn't be forgotten.

Since the boom in sex magazines, that other source of vicarious erotic pleasure, men's magazines or pin-up magazines, have borrowed a few ideas from the barrier-breaking techniques of their more expensive and less reputable neighbours on the news-stands. Several now have hotter pictorial content than many sex magazines but are considered free from censorious comment because they allegedly (although this is not the case with many examples) contain a broad spectrum of literary and photographic entertainment with the pin-up only a part of the selling power. In fact, there is little doubt that the more successful men's magazines sell entirely on their nude photography, with the great majority of the textual matter as sexual and titillating as the more obvious visuals. The quieter relation in the family, the 'naturist' magazine that used to be bought by schoolboys and genuine nudists, has also hotted itself up and some editions of *Health and Efficiency* and *Outdoor Leisure* contain full-frontal photographs, and have done for some considerable while, that are as erotic as those in many sex magazines.

As the sex magazines are the most recent and most overwhelming phenomenon to enter the porn stakes, we might look at them in some detail, although some may well be defunct by the time this is read. The first sex magazine was *Forum,* which was originally published about five years ago as an offshoot of the letters pages of *Penthouse* magazine, which had achieved a notoriety as a sounding-board for all sorts of fantasies about corporal punishment, pubic depilation, circumcision, nipple rings and various fetishist activities. *Forum* added a few short articles mostly of a Freudian psychiatric nature and was sold on subscription only. A couple of years later a magazine called *Curious* appeared, with the at the time innocuous-seeming but in retrospect highly significant aim of providing 'sex education for adults'. Whereas *Forum* was a small-format, black and white, all-text magazine, *Curious* was the usual shape, had plenty of colour and lots of photographs. Then *Forum* went on open sale, and a year later the explosion came. At the end of 1970, *Scorpio* magazine appeared, the third sex magazine on the market and one that took yet a third stance: its sub-title was 'Explorations in Sexuality' and at first it was an uneasy mixture of sociological-styled articles, erotic photographs and speculative features. Immediately after came *Search,* this time taking the cue from *Forum* rather than *Curious.* A host of others followed, lining up either with *Curious-Scorpio* or *Forum-Search,* and with titles like *In Depth, Open, Heat, New Directions, Mentor, Adam, Fringe* (newspaper-format, this one).

Prosecutions against these have been rare. *Curious* was summonsed and fined £50, but had to agree to submit all copy to counsel prior to publication. As a result, it cooled down considerably and for a while took about a 15 per cent drop in sales. Nearly all of this type of magazine claim to be offering sex education (*Scorpio* is the only one that rejects the label), clearly from legal considerations: the breakthrough in sex movies a couple of years ago came with the so-called sex education films, and publishers hoped the same would apply to the printed word. And it's here that the line between magazines and books again gets a bit blurred, for concurrent with the sex education explosion in mags was the mushrooming of books with the same aim—mainly photo books dealing with sex positions. There were several called, simply, *Love Positions,* while others had titles like *The Illustrated Kama Sutra, Sexual Harmony, Sexual Ecstasy* and so on. The first-named of these gives another clue to the real breakthrough in sex magazines and books—the translations of the Eastern love manuals that appeared in the early sixties. They first caused a stir back in the 1880s (see *Victoriana*) and it was the same Burton translations that caused the uproar ten years ago. Incidentally, also on the publishers' lists in the Victorian era were titles like *The Art of Love, Aphrodisiacs, History of the* Rod, *The Lustful Turk,*

Mysteries of Flagellation. All of which are still available, or at least books with the same names are. Magazines of the Victorian era like *The Pearl* were probably more literary and certainly wittier than today's offerings but the state of soft-core porn has remained static. Any basic changes in the business structure of pornography are due to the advent of colour printing and the wider distribution of affluence. Pornography is almost a cottage industry in some parts of London. But the magazine is still a disposable commodity; the book is a permanent thing (see *Books*). This is one factor that suggests that the sex magazine business may collapse somewhat sooner than book publishing. Of course, in general, the same people are behind both, so they don't actually lose, but a magazine without much editorial direction (and sex mags, with a few notable exceptions, don't really seem to have much direction at all) can't survive all that long. Theoretically, a successful magazine is one that establishes an identity and keeps to it; the vagaries of sexual appetite are such that any erotica or pornography must change six-monthly. Hard-core porn magazines do just this and are hardly magazines, they appear and disappear so fast. The rest—well, either they'll have to do a *Men Only* and revamp their whole style every so often or, like all porn, they will disappear quite possibly to reappear with a new name, a new face and a new gimmick (see also *Underground* and *Oz Trial*).

MALCOLM MUGGERIDGE: The following is the text of a speech delivered by Malcolm Muggeridge to the Second Annual Convention of Mary Whitehouse's National Listeners' and Viewers' Association in May 1967. In retrospect, the speech is one of the key events in the current campaign against pornography in Britain.

'I am absolutely convinced that our civilisation will rush down the Gadarene slope which others have slipped down before, if we adhere to the notion that the image of life is not God but pigs in a trough. If life is pigs in a trough, if the purpose of it is to get as much as you can out of the trough, to bury your snout into it, then of course it does not matter much what you show on TV. But all that is just nothing at all.

'If that were life, if *Till Death Us Do Part* is life, really life, I cannot see that there would be anything to do but commit suicide. If that were life. But it is not, and what is needed on the part of people like us, is to have the voice, the inspiration, the clarity of mind, to make people see that it is not life; that all this wretched wallowing about does not even make you happy, doesn't even work.

'You would think that the way to happiness was that everyone should be able to have an abortion, just when she wants it; that marriage should be terminable at will; that contraception should be available to adolescents. You would think that these three things are the secret of happiness.

'Funnily enough this is supposed to be a scientific age, yet if you go to those places where these things are most available, these are the places where the psychiatric wards are fullest, where people are most miserable, where the art is just a nightmare, and where you have a materialistic society.

'If we mean business about this, it is not merely protesting, though I think protest is justifiable in certain circumstances—we have to fix our eyes, our thoughts and our voices on the other side, on the other world—the other world which makes all this seem the tenth-rate, boring despicable thing it is ...

'We are in a situation where our civilisation is running down at such a rate, at a fantastic speed, and the only alternative that I have got is this Christian view of life. If there are others I have not discovered them.

'We shall either succeed in recapturing the incredible magic enchantment of that view of life—away from the trough, away from the dark, dark cell of the ego, away from the idea which is propounded by every one of these media—that happiness lies in being rich and indulging our appetites—either we offer this alternative and somehow recover the captivating quality, or our civilisation will be doomed. I am absolutely certain.

'And I think of a man who has become my hero—a little known Christian, a saint called Paulinus. He lived in the fourth century, at a very similar time, as a matter of fact. A man of great intelligence, he looked at all this permissive morality which was in full cry—circuses, very similar to television, cheap food, welfare, plenty of higher education, and he decided that the only thing he could do was to light a little lamp in a shrine and keep it burning.

'That man is my hero, and I think it is all we can do. If the light does not go out, if the dark ages do not come, there is still a little lamp burning, and it does not show much. But if the darkness does come, then it is bright. When the last dark ages began most people did not know that some obscure events had taken place in a very remote part of the Empire, concerning an extremely unimportant people, events so unimportant that they were unrecorded.

'Yet those events were to be the basis of a civilisation which has lasted nearly two thousand years, and it has been the greatest the world has ever known, and to which we belong.'

MARY WHITEHOUSE, ex-schoolteacher, poetess, co-founder of the 'Clean-Up-TV Campaign' (later to become the National Viewers' and Listeners' Association), friend and ally of Malcolm Muggeridge and Lord Longford, crusader against the 'disbelief, doubt and dirt' she and Mrs Norah Buckland, a rector's wife, (plus, at the time of their petition to Parliament in 1965, 485,000 others) feel that television is pouring out into the living rooms of the nation.

The case against Mary Whitehouse is simple. It is that, while opposing censorship, fighting for more public participation in the media, denouncing the monolithic and unresponsive structure of the BBC, and exposing examples of bias and distortion on the box, she is actually running a personal moral crusade which condemns out of hand everything that offends her own standards of morality, uses smear tactics to discredit 'intellectuals' and 'progressives' (the quotation marks are hers), is the true heir of Moral Rearmament in the 1950s, and suffers from serious delusions of social decay—in other words, she thinks the lesson of history is that pornography leads to the decline and fall, not only of Empires, but of ex-Empires and second-class powers as well.

Since the resignation of her arch enemy, Sir Hugh Carleton Greene, as Director General of the BBC in July 1968 (he described her early campaign as 'the lunatic fringe'), she has put less emphasis on television and more on the whole range of media and the general question of 'pornography' (the quotation marks are ours) in this country. At the same time she has come in from the cold – no longer a provincial prophet crying in the Midlands, she is accepted by the Establishment, the friend of peers and bishops, honoured, when her autobiography was published in 1971, by a literary luncheon at Foyles' Bookshop.

Katherine Whitehorn said of her in *The Observer*:

> 'The real trouble is that she doesn't seem to be able to tell the difference between a sensitive documentary about being a homosexual, a film with bedding and bleeding used alternately for effect, and someone saying 'git' in *Till Death Do Us Part*.'

Discrimination, it's true, has never been her strong point. Neither, for all her many thousands of words about the 'delicacy of minds and hearts' has sensitivity. Many of the stories she tells in her two books about the effects of television on children are horrifying – but not in the way she thinks. For instance, the mother who visited her when she was a teacher. Her daughter had 'gone off with a boy a night or two before'. The girl had been watching TV – 'when it got to the sexy part I could see her getting redder and redder in the face she was so worked up. Then she got up and ran straight out of the house and went off with this boy.' Mrs Whitehouse asked the mother what time her daughter was normally expected to be in. 'But I don't let her out at night because she's too young to be going off with the lads,' the mother told her.

And that is supposed to be a story about the effects of *television*?

She worships authority. All the men in her autobiography were 'towers of strength' to her at one time or another. She recounts, with the zest of the women's magazines, her meetings with MPs, bishops and the like. Officials, especially government officials, are always 'desperately tired but extremely courteous' or walk 'erect and with great dignity'. Her first broadcast, in 1953, was when she sent 'a housewife's thoughts on the eve of the Coronation' to Woman's Hour:

'During the next weeks and months I thought a great deal about what the Queen had said and wondered how someone like myself, so far removed from her as a person, could really help her.' It was to the Queen too that Mrs Whitehouse's first mass meeting in Birmingham sent its resolution: 'To banish from our homes and theatres those who seek to demoralise and corrupt young people.'

Her husband, Ernest, has said of her:

To put it bluntly, we are Christians, and as Christians we do God's will, not our own. It was God's will that Mary should do this work. I had no particular conviction that it was for me to do. My conviction was to support. (*Sunday Express*, 5 September 1971.)

He also described his early meeting with Mary in the following terms—'When I arrived the man she was engaged to was there.' Mary: 'And he left as soon as Ernest came in the door. I said to him later: "Why ever did you go?" and he said: "I realised as soon as Ernest walked in that he was where your heart lay." ' (ibid).

MASOCHISM and **sadism** are the two sides of the same coin and are a perfect example of activities that are considered acceptable in sex until they become obsessive, or physically harmful. Sadism is not necessarily the same as cruelty but is clearly linked to aggression. It is generally considered that it becomes a perversion when sexual satisfaction is impossible without the idea of domination. Masochism is the reverse of this. In fact, pornography tends to concentrate more on masochism than sadism, and the cliché of the voluptuous lady in leather boots, possibly mask and belt, wielding a whip, is still the most common form of middle-range pornography and has hardly changed since Victorian days. Flagellation is the most widely-known of sado-masochistic activities. Soft-core pornographic exploitation of sado-masochism usually includes elements that appeal to the non-sado-masochist, and thus they reap maximum audiences: both parties, sadist-figure and masochist-figure, are often female, and breast-fetishism, buttock-fetishism, leather and rubber-fetishism, not to mention lesbianism and optimum exposure of genitalia, are evident in the most available examples—common in men's magazines as much as in sex mags and pornography and an established part of advertising and marketing techniques and of the popular entertainments scene.

NEVILLE, RICHARD: editor of *OZ* magazine. The following is his speech to the jury during the *OZ* trial the in summer of 1971:

'I suspect the judicial system in this country may not be adequate to comprehend the spirit of this case. I know members of the legal profession care a great deal about the law, but I wonder how *many* of them care about people? Perhaps the law is too important to be left *entirely* to lawyers.

'In this context I should mention the Annual Report of the National Council of Civil Liberties which states that most lawyers in this country are indifferent to what is described in the report as the "drift towards tyranny".

'Now I agree with the remarks made yesterday by My Lordship and by Mr Mortimer about the seriousness of this case. And I think its gravity is not unconnected with the danger of this drift towards tyranny becoming a stampede.

'Some of our most basic freedoms are being whittled away ... bit by bit. The right to strike is in jeopardy. With the Industrial Relations Bill, such accepted practices as the blacking of goods and the sympathy strikes, will become illegal. Of course the right to work itself is in jeopardy too—which at this moment is arousing great anger on Clydeside. Members of the Jury, with the new Immigration Bill, black citizens will actually be required to carry passes, to be produced on demand. Yesterday, outside this very court we have already seen black people cry out against what they regard as rampant injustices. None of these threats to freedom may yet apply to you personally. But those of us in the dock are aware of them all the time. The misuse of the Drugs Bill has given police even more power to search and interfere with the activities of young people. Underground magazines and newspapers—which, as has been explained, are not really so underground—have been persistently harassed by authorities. Three days ago police raided, yet again, the offices of our friendly rival, *International Times*.

'It comes as no surprise to us that the National Council of Civil Liberties accuses the police squads of political censorship in their efforts to suppress magazines like ours.

'We should be on guard against those who seek to close down political discussion under the guise of its so-called obscenity. Every day there are new examples of erosions of liberties, which are all connected with the current economic, moral and political climate.

'Last weekend, a pacifist lawyer of many years standing, David Dellinger, was refused entry into this country. This man is well known for his gentle demeanour and intense hatred of violence in all its forms, which is why he has provided great inspiration to those who oppose the wars in Vietnam, Laos, and Cambodia. He wished to come to this country to visit his teenage daughter—and was refused permission to enter. Such is the price of being a pacifist today.

'Perhaps you may have seen last Friday night's television film about Emile Zola. A timely reminder that after he had been gaoled by a French court for his attempts to reopen the famous Dreyfus case, Zola fled to England where he successfully continued his campaign to get justice done. I am glad that Emile Zola didn't wait until 1971 to seek refuge in England because nowadays he would not be allowed in ... what is worse, very few people would care.

'*OZ* is a magazine which does care about such issues. I first became involved in it with friends in Australia in 1963 and it became the country's best known satirical magazine in 1967, and has since emerged as a regular forum for a wide variety of differing opinions. It is not committed to be rigidly and destructively anti-society, nor does it merely mirror the prejudices of its editors, but *OZ* has become the sounding board for people with new things to say and nowhere else to say them.'

OZ 28 was only one issue in a series, he said. It gave free expression to minority groups.

'There has been a Homosexual *OZ*—edited by homosexuals for the usual *OZ* readership, a Women's liberation *OZ*—edited by Germaine Greer, a women's liberationist, and distributed to the usual *OZ* readership. There has been a Flying Saucer *OZ*—edited not by men from Mars, but by people who believe in such things and the issue was sold to the usual *OZ* readership.

'The Schoolkids' *OZ* was a logical extension of this technique. Perhaps when this trial is over, we can ask you all to edit a Juror's *OZ* ... which like all the others, will be distributed to the usual *OZ* readership.

'But even all these *OZ*es should not be seen in isolation from other magazines and newspapers published in this country such as *International Times, Friends, INK, Mole Express, Styng, Press Ups* and dozens of others, known generally, if misleadingly, as the Underground Press—papers which offer a platform to the socially impotent, and which mirror the changing way of life in our community.

'Because this Underground or Alternative Press is a world-wide phenomenon and because it represents the voice of progress and change in our society, then it is not really only us who are on trial today ... but all of you ... and the right of all of you to freely discuss the issues which concern you.

'Unless I can make it clear, the context in which *OZ* is published, and the culture which has produced this magazine and hundreds like it, then there is the possibility that some of you may have been shocked by it. When you were first given this exhibit to read, some of your hair may have stood on end. Fortunately hair standing on end does not—I'm told—constitute a legal definition of obscenity.

'Over the next few days I hope you may come to understand what *OZ* represents and what *OZ* tries to do. In fact, if we can articulate our beliefs with any force in this court-room we hope that, by the end of this trial, you may become regular subscribers to *OZ* (admittedly it would be a little easier from our point of view if some of you were *already* regular subscribers).

'There are many groups today who are making demands for freedom. These demands of course frighten the established order and I think the charges against me result partly from such fear. This is not surprising. Many people were frightened by the call to abolish slavery and they put forward all sorts of arguments as to why such abolition would lead to the decline and fall of our civilisation.

'Many people say similar things about the current demands for children's rights. Just as many people hotly opposed the idea of women ever having the vote.

'During this case we shall hear more about the increasing agitation of children and the relevance and importance of their demands for all of us. If their demands strike you as impudence, remember that children do not even have the most basic freedoms. They do not have freedom of dress or appearance. They do not have freedom to participate significantly in deciding what they should learn. They do not have freedom of expression—this incident reported last week is typical: A schoolboy claimed in his school magazine that the meals were unhygienic. Instead of answering the allegations, the headmaster merely confiscated all the copies of the magazine and tore off the front page which contained the offending story. That example may seem rather trivial ... but how would you like to be treated like that? What if you published a letter in a local paper attacking the council and the mayor came along and ripped the offending pages out of every copy?

'There was also the case of the young teacher in Stepney – evidently very popular – who had to borrow money in order to publish his pupils' poems. He then got sacked for his pains. Another boy, called Martin Woodhams, got sentenced to a caning when he expressed his frustrations and dreams in a school essay. Martin refused the cane and was punished by suspension.

'Against this essay, the headmaster used the all-purpose excuse of every censor – that the essay was obscene.

'One of the reasons we invited adolescents to edit a special issue of *OZ* was to combat this tendency for everyone to try and shut them up. We were interested in what they had to say. But we didn't want to be like the headmasters who censor everything they don't happen to agree with.

'So we advertised in Issue 26 for any schoolchildren between the ages of 14 and 18 to come and edit *OZ*. We offered them freedom from editorial interference, and we kept our promise. As the prosecution witness, Vivian Berger, has shown – there was no coercion of any kind and our assistance and advice was confined almost exclusively to technical matters. They would not be caned or sent to Coventry if we didn't like what they wrote or drew. *OZ* 28 is the result of this experiment. "Schoolkids" Issue' it says on the cover – which means of course, the issue *edited* by school children, not aimed at them.

'The Prosecution's case assumes that the children wished only to implant lustful and perverted desires. But most of the articles have little to do with sex and are concerned to question authoritarian attitudes on many subjects. The article entitled Weekend Drop Out, is a sensitive and coherent call to reform the school system. I draw your attention especially to the illustration under the heading "School Atrocities", of a teacher molesting a boy, which seems to sum up all the suppressed violence and hypocrisy of institutions.

'"SADISM IN *OZ*" said the headlines 2 nights ago, after the prosecutor's speech. Is this sadistic? Is it not the *behaviour* it depicts which is sadistic? This illustration surely communicates disgust and abhorrence at such practices.

'This magazine consists of 48 pages, including the front and back cover. Like most magazines, it is a mixture of the original and the derivative ... some bits boring, others fascinating, some bits solemn, others satirical ... corny in some places, crude in others ... all in all a gutsy and entertaining read for 20 pence. It contains varied attacks on accepted attitudes, which as far as I know is not yet against the law ... in fact it contains varied attacks on *OZ* Magazine itself, which I doubt can be the cause of this prosecution.

'But remember, if you convict us at the end of this trial, you are in reality convicting schoolchildren. And if you convict schoolchildren, then you yourselves must accept some responsibility for their guilt.

'However, so far from debauching and corrupting the morals of children and young persons within the realm, our evidence will show that *OZ* is part of a communications network which intends the very opposite. It sets out to enlighten and to elevate public morals.

'On the charge of publishing an obscene magazine, I just wish to say that this court will benefit from a great deal of new evidence which has come to light in recent years. On 30 September 1970, the most comprehensive report on obscenity and pornography ever undertaken in the world recommended to the US Congress that "all federal, state and local legislation prohibiting the sale, exhibition and distribution of sexual material to consenting adults" should be repealed. A possible distinction between sexual offenders and other people with regard to explicit sexual material while maturing. This Report includes a thorough breakdown of Danish statistics which reveals beyond any doubt that sex crimes in Denmark have dropped since the abolition of obscenity laws ... one reason why, of course, Sweden has since followed suit.

'This report deals with the sort of porno magazines which are so important to the economy of Soho—not with the magazines of such diverse interests as *OZ*. Two of the Commissioners make a special point about children. "There is no substantial evidence that exposure to juveniles is necessarily harmful," they write. "There may even be beneficial effects if for no other reason than the encouragement of open discussions about sex between parents and children relatively early in young lives."

'That such discussion about sex between parents and young people is urgently overdue is brought vividly to light in the current case of the 12-year-old pregnant girl. The mother has already said, she blames herself for not being able to talk to her child easily about sex. It is characteristic of authorities in this country that MPs are already calling for the boy to be punished instead of trying to understand the real cause of the tragedy ... the growing IGNORANCE GAP between parents and children. Schoolkids' *OZ* was a step in the direction of closing that gap.

'Now the conspiracy charge against us is acutely serious ... it is not pleasant to be accused of debauching and corrupting the morals of young persons, even though, as John Mortimer has pointed out, it was once applied to Socrates ... But at the same time there is an element of absurdity in the indictment because over the next few days we will establish beyond any reasonable doubt that the charge is thoroughly unfounded ... and the real seriousness of the charge is not so much that we three are in the dock defending it, but that the Director of Public Prosecutions has the cynical effrontery to resurrect it from some ill-begotten statute.

'We regard it as a serious travesty of our liberties—and indeed your liberties—that this magazine has been continually harassed by police—as Detective Inspector Frederick Luff virtually admitted two days ago. We regard it as a travesty that we are being called upon to defend our attempts to communicate with one another.

'You see, we think it would make more sense if it was the Home Secretary in the dock. For we should ask you to convict him of violating our freedom of expression or, in this case, violating our freedom to allow teenagers to express themselves.

'Do you remember the fairy tale about the Emperor with no clothes. How the Emperor paraded the streets naked, deluding himself that he had a suit of fine new cloth, and how the only one of his subjects with the security, courage and honesty to expose him was a "young person within his realm". In many ways our society today is naked, obscenely naked at that. The real obscenities in this world—the causes of true depravity and corruption—are things such as poverty, war, homelessness, and greed.

'Yet this trial is brought by the leaders of our obscene society. Not only does our Emperor deny that he is naked, but he drags his young accusers into court on the charge of them being corrupters and debauchers.'

OBSCENE PUBLICATIONS ACT of 1959: highly complex act which was originally intended to simplify things. Sponsored by Roy Jenkins inside Parliament and the Society of Authors outside, the Act provided the first effective defence against a charge of obscenity:

> A person shall not be convicted of an offence against section two of this act and an order for forfeiture shall not be made under the foregoing section if it is proved that publication of the article in question is justified as being for the public good on the ground that it is in the interests of science, literature, art or learning, or of other objects of general concern.

The history of the Act is the history of this defence in a decade of major 'show trials' from *Lady Chatterley* (1960) to *Oz* (1971).

All went well until the trial of *Last Exit to Brooklyn* (1965). Up to that date, the defence provided under the Act seemed triumphant. In every case, the prosecution had the greatest difficulty in finding any witnesses (only four independent prosecution witnesses have appeared in trials under the Act: three in the *Last Exit* case and one – Vivian Berger, who turned out to be a hostile witness – in *Oz*. Set against this the veritable army of experts who have appeared for the defence). The only conviction was in the case against *Fanny Hill* where the prosecution attempted to use a *different* section of the Act – Section 3, providing for rapid action against booksellers, rather than publishers – to bring a case against a book in the magistrates' court, thus allowing of no proper defence by the publishers, Mayflower, who weren't even called. By charging an arbitrary bookseller, a Mr Gold, with possession of obscene articles for gain, the prosecution in effect established that *Fanny Hill* was obscene. The result was the 1964 Parliamentary amendment which allowed the defence in cases under Section 3, brought in a magistrates' court, to appeal for trial by jury and to claim the same justification of publication 'in the interests of science, literature, art, or ... general concern'.

It is only when we come to *Last Exit* and to *Oz* that the long history of defence success falters. In both these cases, convictions were obtained and only put aside on appeal. In both cases, John Mortimer, QC, defended and appealed. And in both cases the grounds for the appeal were *virtually identical*:

1. In both cases, the judge failed to give proper weight in his summing up to the defence theory of aversion: namely, that the material in question was not obscene because it would shock or horrify the average reader and, far from deprave or corrupting him, inoculate him through aversion against depravity and corruption.
2. In both cases, the judge failed to define the Act's test of obscenity correctly. The act states 'an article shall be deemed obscene if its effect or (where the article comprises two or more distinct items) the effect of any one of its items is, if taken as a whole, such as to deprave and corrupt persons who are likely, having regard to all relevant circumstances to read, see or hear the matter contained in it.'

In the *Last Exit* case, while quoting dictionary definitions of 'deprave' and 'corrupt' correctly, the judge failed to give these words their full meaning, namely that reading the book would lead to immoral *action,* not just thoughts or intentions. He also failed to define 'persons' correctly as a significant proportion of the people who might reasonably be expected to read the book (a different thing from the public at large); and he failed to define properly the defence of the 'public good'. This defence, which only becomes a matter for consideration if the jury have first concluded that the article in question *is* obscene, is, according to the Appeal Court, a matter of the jury weighing in their mind the factors for and against the book's publication and deciding *on balance* if publication is in the public interest: an easier defence than if they had to decide, for example, whether or not the book was in itself a great work of literature before clearing it.

In the *Oz* trial the judicial error was rather more startling. Judge Argyle actually widened the definition of 'obscenity' by quoting not only the Act, but the dictionary, thus giving the jury the impression that they could convict an article because it was 'lewd' or 'revolting' or 'disgusting'. The test of obscenity in the Act is much more technical and much tougher than this.

It is only with Lord Widgery's judgment on the *Oz* appeal that we at last have a clear picture of the judicial interpretation of the 1959 Act. Even after the *Last Exit* appeal, confusion continued For example, it should have been clear after that case that expert witnesses could only be called to dispute Section 4: whether or not the book had redeeming merits re science, literature, art or the public good. They could not be called to testify on the actual issue of whether or not the article in question was obscene or did deprave and corrupt. They would then be pre-empting the task of the jury. Yet this is precisely what most of the defence witnesses in the *Oz* case were there for. It's true that a minor case against the 'ABC Chewing Gum' company had muddled the issue. In that case, concerning some 'horror comic' cards given away with bubblegum, an appeal court overruled the acquittal of ABC because the lower court had refused the prosecution the right to call experts (psychiatrists) to testify as to whether or not the cards could harm children collecting them. But, as Lord Widgery has now pointed out in his judgment on *Oz*, the case is one of 'limited precedent' since the psychology of very young children at issue there was a matter on which a judge or a jury could expect guidance.

The *Oz* case has also been a classic for two other reasons. Judge Argyle accepted the defence contention that the magazine be judged as a whole, which he shouldn't have done. More important, it was the first trial in which the Obscene Publications Act was used with a moral conspiracy charge. This is an altogether different sort of charge, and much more difficult to defend. With its origins in the Court of Star Chamber, 'conspiracy' has always been a 'catch-all' charge under common law (i.e. the law made by judges and precedents rather than by act of parliament), a reservoir for the power of the State. It has an obvious use in criminal law, where two men might be caught planning a bank robbery but before the robbery could be committed. But its extension to the field of public morals in the 1961 Shaw case is much more controversial. Shaw was a publisher who produced a directory of prostitutes in the early 1960s. He appealed against conviction on a 'conspiracy to corrupt public morals' charge. The case went to the Lords where the conviction was upheld. In a memorable debate which produced classic statements on the role of the law in regard to morals, Lord Simonds put this view:

> In the sphere of criminal law, there remains in the Courts of law a residual power to enforce the supreme and fundamental purpose of the law to conserve not only the safety and order but also the moral welfare of the State, and it is our duty to guard

> it against attacks which might be all the more insidious because they were novel and unprepared for ... it matters little what label is given to the offending act—an affront to public decency, a corruption of public morals, the creation of a public mischief or the undermining of moral conduct.

In reply, Lord Reid put the opposing case:

> There are wide differences of opinion today as to how far the law ought to punish immoral acts which are not done in the face of the public. Parliament is the proper and only place to settle that. When there is sufficient support from public opinion, Parliament does not hesitate to intervene. Where Parliament fears to tread, it is not for the courts to rush in.

In the *Oz* case, the dangerous precedent of combining a conspiracy charge with a charge under the Obscene Publications Act seems to have been established. Although *Oz* was acquitted on the morals charge it is difficult to believe that testimony on that charge—so much looser, so much more wide-ranging, totally without any of the complex technical limitations of the Obscene Publications Act—didn't affect the jury's decision on the obscenity charge. How any jury in the future could possibly keep clear and distinct in their minds the testimony on two such unrelated, even diametrically opposed, charges in terms of the evidence required to prove them, God only knows.

'Conspiracy' was also the issue in the other major morals case in recent years: the case against *International Times*. Convicted fo publishing small ads for all kinds of sexual activity including homosexuality, their case was on appeal to the House of Lords who thu had an opportunity to reverse their Shaw decision. Undoubtedly under current law, *IT* was rightly convicted. Homesexuality wa in fact specifically mentioned in the Shaw debate when Viscoun Simonds said,

> Let us suppose, My Lords, that at some future, perhaps early date homosexual practices between consenting adults are n longer a crime. Would it not be an offence if even withou obscenity such practices were publicly advocated and encourage by pamphlet and advertisement? Or must we wait until Parliamen finds time to deal with such conduct? I say, My Lords, that if th

common law is powerless in such an event then we should no longer do her reverence.

(This quotation was cited in the *IT* judgment.)

The appeal decision on the *IT* case has so far not been encouraging. In a wide-ranging judgment, the Appeal Court has virtually made it illegal for anyone to advertise for another person for sexual purposes. Yet many lawyers dispute the whole basis of the Shaw debate. They argue that, if it is corrupting public morals to advertise homosexuality, surely it must be corrupting public morals to consent to a homosexual act. Thus the parliamentary exception to the laws against homosexuality, made for consenting adults in private, could in theory be wiped out by a morals charge.

This, then, is the current state of the law on Obscene Publications – confused and contradictory.

In addition, we have the Post Office Act (where the test of obscenity is very different and involves only that the article should be 'lewd' and 'disgusting' – the dictionary definition, in fact. And what magazine or book isn't sent through the post at some stage?); and the catch-all charges of conspiring to corrupt public morals, against which there can be very little defence and certainly no defence on the grounds of 'science, art, literature'. (There is a possible, though untested defence of the 'public good'. If it could be shown that a conspiracy was in the public good, it could not be injurious to public morals.) The fear is that, after a decade of trials in which the accused has come off best, the prosecution may begin to shift its ground and bring increasing numbers of charges outside the Obscene Publications Act, or employ the Act in tandem with more ill-defined 'offences'.

Yet the question of obscenity and the law is not, in the end, a legal one. Any law is only effective in so far as it is enforced and the real complaint about the law as it relates to morals is the State's choice of people to prosecute. On the whole the professional publishers of girlie magazines and sex books go free. Soho flourishes. Occasionally someone is hauled in for overstepping the mark and a small fine goes unnoticed in a paragraph in *The Times*. In no way does that compare with Detective Inspector Luff's and Judge Argyle's views of *Oz* or with the astonishingly virulent appeal court ruling against *IT*. It seems that sex, please, we're British, is acceptable. It is the rise of the 'underground' with their use of sex combined with revolutionary rhetoric, the linking of a free and open sexuality with radical politics, which is the real target of the forces of law and order. And 'pornography' and 'obscenity' are just convenient pegs to hang *IT* on.

OBSESSIONS: The pornography that seems to arouse most hostility is that which shows 'sexual perversions' such as bestiality, sado-masochism and fetishism. At the very root of pornography, of course, is voyeurism (in the buyer) and to a lesser extent exhibitionism (in the models). 'Perversions', 'abnormalities', 'deviant behaviour', call them what you will, are minority interests and it is hardly surprising that certain outlets exist for the satisfaction of these interests; the interests are not only minority ones but also mostly illegal and so the catering for these tastes must necessarily be clandestine. It is generally agreed that most of us have the potentiality to become 'kinky' but we either don't have that particular nerve exposed or we are aware of it and control it (with perhaps greater neurotic damage). The point where 'peeping' becomes voyeurism and where showing off becomes indecent exposure or exhibitionism is when the activity becomes an obsession.

Pin-up magazines, commercial movies and pulp fiction all cater for the fascination with fetishism and the mild flirtation many people have with deviance. The emphasis on sado-masochism is quite evident from *The Avengers* and James Bond to leather fashions and sauna baths, and various other less common deviations have been touched upon in the media and entertainments industries, for example bestiality (most explicit in Pasolini's *Pigsty*; and there's female masturbation of animals in Chaucer and in Beardsley's unfinished novel *Under the Hill*, fetishism (knicker-type in *The Anniversary*, a play and a movie, and since invariably recurring in umpteen sexploitation movies), buggery (hardly a perversion although our forebears thought so and still certainly a serious crime referred to jocularly by the Restoration poets, passionately by D. H. Lawrence and John Cowper Powys), flagellation (which abounds in Victorian pornography as well as in authors like Swinburne and Monckton Milnes and is one of the principal sources of erotic today, although usually implied rather than explicit) and voyeurism-exhibitionism. (Many so-called movie documentaries rely on a voyeurist obsession.) (See also *Cunnilingus*: and *Masochism*.)

Would you photograph leather or sado-masochist books? Yes, I would actually. Because I've sat in sex bookshops and their most dedicated customers come in with half a dozen sado-masochist books under their arm and swap them for another six and go away and they're all terribly respectable people. They've just got this hangup. Far better they should buy the books than go around looking for people to beat. It's very important those books should be about. I feel very strongly about this – also I think people who confuse that with violence are absolutely bonkers. Everybody seems to, and it isn't the same thing at all. Violence in sex books doesn't sell. You very rarely see rape in sex books for example.

Tuppy Owens, freelance sex photographer and author of *Love in the Open Air*.

Two or three years ago we made a serious mistake. We decided that with all this porn about and so on society must be becoming sexually much more sophisticated. So we moved into doing speciality books – like the *Sweet Smell of Sex* which was about, well, pongs. Then along came this simple Love Position book and we sold half a million. And suddenly you realise that the problem isn't people who aren't getting wet lettuces thrown at them while they dress up in frogmen's suits, the problem is that most people still aren't getting it at all.

Len Holdsworth of Charles Skilton's Luxor Books, a leading sex book imprint.

OH, CALCUTTA! Opened in New York in June 1969, and in London a year later. Kenneth Tynan, who devised it, with many a witty writer said to have contributed though critics wondered where, explained in the *Village Voice*.

Some time ago, it occurred to me that there was no place for a civilised man to take a civilised woman to spend an evening of civilised erotic stimulation. At one end there's burlesque, at the other an expensive night club, but no place in between. We're trying to fill that gap with this show.

Unkind observers wondered about Mr Tynan's bank balance and some were disappointed by the sketches frequently carried out in the nude, though Clive Barnes and his celebrated 'it gives pornography a bad name' apart, there was heady praise for the naked 'funky country blues pas de deux' and its 'joyous interweaving of these beautiful bodies.' (Jack Kroll in *Newsweek*.)

Tynan also said:

> We're asking [the public] to respond in public to things which they usually respond to in private. There is no theatrical consensus yet as to how to respond to sex; no one knows how he feels about watching people make love. So every night we have an experimental laboratory in people's reaction to sex on the stage.

Gillian Hanson in her book *Original Skin*, is in favour:

> The importance of the show is in its total nudity, in the use of the human body in a number of strange, joyful, pitiful and erotic ways and the audiences running the gamut of interest, excitement, embarrassment, fear and identification—just what tragedy used to arouse before the theory of psychoanalysis taught the world that there is no innocent action, no unselfish motive—and no blame.

Gosh!

The cast may occasionally have complained of the cold and a team of jokes emerged about stand-ins. Other complaints were more volatile. The intrepid dissenting commissioner Charles Keating of the American Commission on Obscenity and Pornography, wrote

> It is not possible to verbally depict the depravity, deviation eroticism or the utter filth of the play. Male and female players fondle each other, commit or simulate intercourse, sodomy cunnilingus, masturbation, sadism, *ad nauseam*. This abomination at the time I write this Report, is proposed to be televised live or by video tape across the nation via lines of American Telephone and Telegraph and various telephonic communications systems Never in Rome, Greece, or the most debauched nation in history has such utter filth been projected to all parts of a nation.

N.B. for those who have forgotten, *Oh, Calcutta!* does have witt connexions. The term is a pun on the French: *O! quel cul tu as* or 'Oh, what an arse you've got!'.

OZ TRIAL (1971): Uniquely significant trial under the Obscene Publications Act because it brought together such disparate and controversial elements as the relation of sex and politics, the legal limits of the Obscene Publications Act, and the division between the young and old generations. It was also the first major obscenity trial which resulted in a guilty verdict since pre-*Lady Chatterley* days (1960). While *Oz* magazine continued publication with a soaring circulation after the trial (an interesting and by no means single instance of the double-edged effectiveness of censorship), there were grounds for thinking its great days were over. At its peak, the magazine pioneered the use of 'obscenity' for broadly political purposes. Most of its individual articles were mediocre. Together they added up to a manifesto for political and social revolution whose importance only became clear to many people with the trial and Richard Neville's speeches in his own defence (see *Neville*). The clashes between Judge Argyle and the defence witnesses and the use of 'conspiracy' as a blanket charge which is almost impossible either to prove or disprove were also revealing features of a case whose implications are only in abeyance till the next time. (See also *Trials* and the *Obscene Publications Act* and *Small Ads*.)

In the excerpts from the trial which follow, Mr Brian Leary was prosecuting counsel and Mr John Mortimer defence counsel.

Mr Leary: Miss Coon, you and I understand one another, do we not?

Caroline Coon (director of 'Release'): Do you honestly expect me to say Yes?

Mr Michael Schofield, Lecturer in Psychology, London University: I sincerely believe that, were it not for the activities of the police, this edition of *Oz* would have been forgotten a very long time ago ...

(Replying to a prosecution question about the Rupert Bear cartoon.) The cartoon is intended to be humorous ... The sexual part in this cartoon is of little importance ... The main point about it is that Rupert Bear is behaving in a way one would not expect a little bear to behave.

Mr Leary: But what sort of *age* would you think Rupert is to your mind; what *sort* of aged bear?

Schofield: I'm very sorry, I'm not up to date with bears.

Mr Leary: You don't have to be, because he doesn't change, does he?

Judge: I think the question is, what age do you think Rupert is intended to be, a child, adult, or what?

Schofield: It's an unreal question. You might as well ask me how old is Jupiter?

Mr Leary: He's a young bear, isn't he? He goes to school—that's right, isn't it?

Schofield: I don't know whether he went to school or not. I'm sorry; but I'm obviously not as well informed as you are about little bears. I'm a psychologist.

Mr Leary (consulting a small ad for a gay person): Does this advertisement not pander to the lust of homosexuals?

Felix Dennis: I find that question repulsive. Would you rephrase it?

Judge: No. Answer it.

Mr Brian Leary: Ask yourselves what good ever came out of *Oz 28*? What lesson is there for us to learn? Members of the Jury, there is none, is there? Save that sex is a god to be worshipped for its own sake; save that doing one's own thing is an ideal to be looked up to by young and old alike no matter how selfish that attitude may be.

It is for you, ladies and gentlemen of this Jury, to set the standard by which we shall continue to live in this country.

Ask yourselves: what is this 'alternative society'? Expecting the State to provide, and by the State, I mean nothing more than you and me, those of us who don't mind working, and who think it's right to work, those of us who are fools enough to work?

It's the stress upon drugs and the stress upon sex, *throughout* this magazine, of which the Crown complains. It is a magazine which after all, finishes with the rhyme: 'There were days I spent in an aggravated haze, and weeks of endless bother. But now I dig the spinach craze, and incest with my mother.' Members of the Jury, that's the magazine which you are asked to consider in the light of what my learned friend, Mr Mortimer said about the right of people to dissent. Members of the Jury, this is not a case about children's right to do anything. This is a case about people publishing that which some people may think should *not* be published.

Members of the Jury, *Oz* 28 is nothing more or less than propaganda. It's not a proper vehicle for the assessment of ideas. Surely, on that first reading of it, it left you with an ugly taste in your mouth. Let me seek to analyse what that taste was; it's the very epitome, is it not, of the so-called permissive society? The idea that experimenting with drugs is all right and that the law is a silly one and shouldn't be complied with; that a man whose job it is to act as a police officer is always aptly called a 'pig'; that sexual freedom is to be encouraged; that everyone should sleep with everyone else as soon as they are able to understand what it is all about; that sexual activity is to be admired for itself; voyeurism, homosexuality, flagellation, necrophilia – making love to a dead person – that's all fun and to be encouraged. And, members of the Jury, there is a further message within the covers of this book: that there is nothing wrong with promiscuity and that if you get venereal disease as a result of promiscuity, that's nothing to be ashamed of. It's just one of the hazards of ordinary normal life, like catching a cold travelling on the Underground. That's why the Crown invites you to look at this particular magazine. This isn't a medical text book. We've been through that magazine from cover to cover and agreed that there is not one word of tenderness expressed within it. That is because this magazine does not deal with love. It deals with sex with a capital 'S'.

The Judge's summing-up was stunning. Suddenly the defence witnesses became 'so-called defence experts', some of whom, Members of the Jury: 'you may think reached the position ... where they either had to admit they were wrong or tell a lie.' If *Oz* was a window on the hippy world – 'well, windows sometimes need cleaning, don't they?' As he finished with a witness, he would toss his copy of *Oz* disdainfully down on to the table, and with it, one felt the case for the defence. It was a distressing and perhaps crucial exercise. For after constant 'exposure to' (a favourite expression of Mr Leary's) 'fucking in the streets', 'masturbation', 'deviation', 'lesbianism', 'corruption', and 'cannabis', this middle-aged group of British householders – the Jury – was asked quite simply 'to set the standard'. What an invitation.

Jonathan Dimbleby on the '*Oz* Trial' in the *New Statesman*.

*P*OLITICS: *There are more things in the Sexual Revolution, Malcolm Muggeridge, than are dealt with in your morality. Or, for that matter, in this book. Our subject is 'obscenity and pornography' and we are perhaps dealing with symptoms rather than causes. The invention of the Pill has, undoubtedly, been more important in releasing the floodtide of 'filth' and 'lax morals' the anti-pornographers feel is engulfing Britain than all the erotic literature in the world. Important too, is the history of modern thought about sexuality, and particularly about sex related to politics. And so, flying about a million miles above the heads of the House of Lords, some thoughts (not ours, we hasten to add) ...*

Sex occupies the same place in modern politics that religion did in the politics of the 16th century. That isn't true, but it's a nice thought. And there are some truths in it. The *Oz* Trial may not be the beginning of the modern Wars of Sexuality, but sexual politics, like religious politics, have their own importance in the realms of political theory and their own power to anger and incite more than politics *per se*. In this century, sex has become a kind of catalyst to revolutionary politics: no one is sure how much they should add or what will happen when they do. Will the resulting mixture turn Karl Marx into Jekyll and Hyde? Hence the caution and circumspection with which older revolutionaries treat the issue of sexual freedom (notoriously, Bolshevik Russia was a puritan state) and the enthusiasm with which it has been seized on by the young.

The connexion of sex and politics rests on two propositions: that sex is the embodiment of freedom and that sexual repression is one of the ways the modern state survives or, at least, declines and falls gracefully. The serious theory of sexual politics has been an attempt to reconcile Marx and Freud. For a long time the attempt was in the hands of a line of intellectuals most people thought of as plain nutty. But as the academic world continues to bash its head against the brick wall of Marxist analysis, it is beginning to favour anyone who might offer a way out.

Wilhelm Reich fell out with Freud in the early 1930s. Along with Rank and Ferenzi, he was involved with the search for a more effective therapy than classic psychoanalysis: the 'talking cure'. The search led Reich to his own theory with its three major components – the theory of the orgasm, the theory of character, and the therapy he was seeking – 'character analysis'. Reich simply approached the problem of neurosis from the opposite end, taking up Freud's distinction between psychoneurosis (neurosis caused by memory), and actual neurosis, which expressed itself in physical symptoms like impotence. A more or less physical illness had a more or less physical cure – hence the paramount importance Reich attached to the orgasm, the release of the most important sort of energy, 'the central regulating mechanism of the closed energy system called man'. (*The Sexual Radicals*, Paul A. Robinson. Paladin Books 1972.) Complementary to this theory of orgasm was the theory of character. Character was now the area where neurosis had its origins, not the Freudian unconscious. And character was of course a repressive force bound up with civilisation and culture.

So far, so Freudian. But Reich broke with Freud over the political implications of psychology. Where Freud argued, in *Civilisation and Its Discontent* that repression and character were unalterable facts of man's nature—man must suppress his instincts to be civilised, but this very suppression creates the neurosis which makes any 'true' or 'perfect' civilisation impossible—Reich moved further towards Marxism. Attempting to reconcile Freud and Marx, he seized on the gap in Marxist analysis between the economic substructure and the ideological superstructure. Marx had argued that this was the result of 'false consciousness'. But what if false consciousness was a psychological reality, what if ideology could be so grafted into the personality that men not only thought differently but *were* different? Reich attacked the family as the unit which passed on ideology from generation to generation (since ideology was always imbibed in childhood, it was naturally always out of date—hence the gap Marx described). And the basis of the family for Reich was sexual repression.

Thus sexual repression became the key element in the repressive society. For psychology read sex. The Freudian corpus, concerned to show man as a sexual being, had been grafted on to Marxism with its concentration on economic man. Both became shorthand for an ultimate freedom. But where, for Freud, repression had been inevitable and basic to any kind of culture, for Reich and the Freudian radicals it was a tool which propped up authoritarian regimes.

Reich failed in all his attempts to get the European Left of the 1930s to adopt sexual liberation as a part of their platform. In 1933, he left Germany, first for Scandinavia, then America. Progressively disillusioned with politics, he turned to biology and spent his last twenty years in elaborating a vast biological and cosmological myth: the 'discovery' of orgasmic energy as a physical substance called 'orgone energy', the 'discovery' of the life force itself.

It was left to Herbert Marcuse in the 1950s to take up and take forward the task of reconciling Freud and Marx. He shared with the other Freudian radicals their dual conviction that Freud's major achievement had been to point out the high price mankind has paid for civilisation and society; and that Freud's major work was his later historical/philosophical books, almost totally ignored by the increasingly respectable and 'medical' psychiatric profession.

Marcuse, in *Eros and Civilisation,* created two concepts which were a marriage of Freud and Marx. 'Surplus Repression'—corresponding to Marx's surplus value—rescued Freud from his own pessimism. Yes, said Marcuse, Freud was right, repression is an essential element in any civilisation, but only a small amount of repression. What we have in modern capitalism is a vast amount of surplus repression—repression that goes, not into creating a culture, but into dominating one. The 'performance principle', corresponding to Marx's alienation and reification theories, was a qualitative measure of the same thing. Freud had stated two principles: the 'pleasure principle' or unrepressed, instinctive behaviour and the 'reality principle' of repressed civilised behaviour. The 'performance principle' was a way of putting the reality principle into historical perspective, and thus integrating it with Marxism. Behaviour was *more* repressed under capitalism, which operated a sort of super-reality principle of its own.

Marcuse shared with Reich his view of the fundamental importance of sexual freedom; but whereas Reich had defined true sexuality as exclusively genital, Marcuse thought it pre-genital, the whole body as an erotic zone (as it is supposed to be in infants). One of Marcuse's most ingenious arguments is that, under capitalism, sexuality has become focused in the genital area, so as to release the rest of the body for productive labour! The second major disagreement between Marcuse and Reich was over the importance of the family. Marcuse felt that the family was no longer an important repressive agent. It had been replaced as the transmitter of ideology – or tradition – by the bureaucracy and the mass media.

The problem of society for Marcuse was to 'resolve the antagonism of sexuality and work'. He had struggled rather unsatisfactorily with Freud's theory of the death instinct. Other Freudian radicals had skirted this awkward theory which seemed to define Freud finally as a political conservative, because a profound pessimist about human nature. Freud had seen life as a struggle between Eros (Sex) and Thanatos (Death). Thanatos led to aggression (fear of death) and the only hope of escaping destruction was by repression which sublimated Eros (Sex) into 'Love' or 'Affection', capable of soothing the savage self-destructive beast that was man. Marcuse chose to regard the Eros/Thanatos struggle as a historical event. The release of Eros – i.e. liberation – would enable sex to fight death and win. The sublimation Freud talked about therefore became a social/historical matter, and in those terms was represented by the idea of work. Marcuse saw two futures for work. First, technology would massively decrease the amount of work necessary; secondly, work itself would move nearer to play and involve some erotic content.

By the 1960s, with the revival of the American Left, Marcuse had returned to his first love – politics. His latest work, like *One-Dimensional Man,* shows a return to political solutions, away from the Utopia of a Freudian-Marxist reconciliation. For example, Marcuse has now turned against technology as a liberating agent and sees current sexual permissiveness as a repressive phenomenon, a reaction of capitalism to include and defuse the liberating force of free sex. With two strokes, Marcuse has thus denied the two most immediate revolutionary forces of *Eros and Civilisation*; and the success of a theoretical Freudian-Marxist coalition thus becomes visionary rather than practical – it has had the skates pulled from under it. On the other hand, Marcuse obviously still longs for some such 'Unpopular Front' and in his view of the youth/black movement as the modern-day Marxist proletariat, there are still elements of sexual liberation and a lingering emphasis on the possible significance of such slogans as 'Make Love, Not War'.

While neither Reich nor Marcuse managed to get sexual liberation built into most political platforms, including most revolutionary ones, their work has been adopted, in a popular and hazy form, by the variety of semi-political bodies known as the 'underground'.

Reich came first. As Robinson points out, the Beat Generation of the 1950s in America was talking a kind of Reichian rhetoric at the same time as they defended a much vaguer idea of sexual freedom than Reich ever could have countenanced. (He regarded homosexuality as a perversion, for example.) And there are traces enough both of Reich and Marcuse in such tracts as Richard Neville's *Playpower* with its vision of work as play, or any underground newspaper in either America or Britain where open sex is juxtaposed with revolutionary politics. 'Juxtaposed' is the right word – the sexual freedom isn't Freudian and the revolution isn't Marxist in any strict sense. Perhaps that is encouraging: while the partners the radical Freudians struggled so hard to marry have blurred their roles, and their quarrels and differences have lost their power to hurt, the memory of their union lingers on.

PORNOGRAPHY: It's commonly assumed that pornography, eroticism and obscenity are interchangeable, or at least that each has a touch of the others. In fact pornography need not be erotic (i.e. arousing); eroticism need not be pornographic and obscenity, of course, need have nothing to do with sex at all. There are many cases of pornographic art that depict sexual activity without any implied or inferred erotic effect, for example some of the drawings of Rembrandt or Mihaly Zichy (see *Erotic Art*), and it is only repressed sexuality and curiosity that makes much other pornographic art also erotic, for example the Hindu temple sculptures. (One might mention here the bizarre case of Sir Francis Dashwood's topiary artifacts near West Wickham's notorious Hell Fire Caves, which reputedly formed pornographic designs when viewed from above: since they were created in the 18th century and were razed to the ground well before the invention of the aeroplane, let alone aerial photography, their erotic intent must have far outstripped their erotic effect!)

Eroticism, similary, needn't be at all pornographic. Rock music is generally regarded as very sexually stimulating on a basic aural level, just as Scriabin's symphonic poems or Beethoven's *Eroica* are, and other aphrodisiacs, from perfumes to drugs, are altogether independent of any graphic depiction of sexual activity.

Of course by etymological definition some writers, and D. H. Lawrence is an obvious example, are pornographers because they write of sexual activity; but we don't call it pornography, we call it literature because literature is what it is first of all, while parts may be pornographic as a secondary consideration (see also *Lawrence*). Non-narrative arts, on the other hand, have to capture one instant and the pornography is thus that much more pornographic. Novels and movies that are pure pornography are usually no more than a series of static tableaux. That's why to write a truly pornographic book or make a pornographic movie is so difficult, and to do it well is very, very difficult. Susan Sontag argues that it can be done.

It's surprising how many writers have written about 'pornography' without attempting to define it. H. Montgomery Hyde in his book *A History of Pornography* has a whole chapter called 'What Is Pornography?' and doesn't manage to give a satisfactory answer. He acknowledges the original Greek ('the writing of harlots'); notes 'hence it has come to mean, in the definition of the Oxford English Dictionary, "the expression or suggestion of obscene or unchaste subjects in literature or art" '; concludes that 'the essential characteristic of a pornographic work is its sexuality' and then, amazingly, comes up with the blatant *non sequitur*, 'therefore, in order to come within the category of pornography, the writing or picture or sculpture must have the power or be intended to act as an aphrodisiac—that is, to excite sexual passions or desires.' Why? Such a definition could only be made in the context of a Western tradition where everything to do with sexual behaviour is considered in the light of its ability to arouse others.

He then goes on to decide that you can't define obscenity at all and yet 'all pornography is obscene'. Thus if you talk about pornography then you are talking about obscenity, itself no more than a legal term, and a pretty vague one at that. The Kronhausens put forward watertight theories, even if they do assign their own meanings to words. Hard-core pornography to them is pure fantasy material, designed primarily for erotic stimulation, while erotic realism, as they call such works as *Lady Chatterley's Lover* and Henry Miller's books, contains 'other considerations which predominate over the sexual contents'. These attempted definitions, however wrong they may be, nevertheless reflect the commonly-held interpretation of pornography: something that is meant to arouse sexually. And maybe this is the least we should settle for; quite what we decide to call the depiction of sexual activity when it isn't meant to arouse—well, in our sort of society the problem rarely arises. But having conceded that common usage has distorted the word to mean something designed to be sexually arousing, this doesn't seem quite the same as obscenity which most would interpret as something revolting. Pornography may be disapproved of because it does arouse, and perhaps the censors do believe that being aroused can lead to moral decadence, to psychological damage and possibly to criminal acts, but that it should be prosecuted as obscene, and even equated with obscenity, would seem to be a contradiction. The celebrated American judgment on Joyce's *Ulysses*, when lifting the censorship on that book, was that the work was 'emetic', a word one might well apply to, say, *Last Exit to Brooklyn* or to de Sade's writings: the right to move the reader to sickness as necessary to the artist as the right to move him to masturbate, or to tears or laughter.

Kinsey asserts that pornography is 'literature or drawing that has the erotic arousal of the reader or observer as its deliberate and primary or sole objective' although he makes it clear that the definition is what is understood rather than its strict meaning. The American sociologist Ned Polsky equates pornography with prostitution in that both are 'different roads to the same end', and that they both 'provide for the discharge of what society calls anti-social sex, i.e. impersonal, non-marital sex'. Pornography provides it via masturbatory, imagined intercourse with a fantasy object. In fact, to Polsky, pornography is simply an aid to masturbation, a dressed-up version of the old definition of 'a book you read with one hand'—and he criticises the Kronhausen theory that there is a difference between hard-core pornography and 'erotic realism': as he says, if a book is declared non-pornographic (that is, if it has literary or other redeeming qualities) you don't stop masturbating to it. In other words, if a work arouses then it's pornographic and if it's good literature to boot then it's even more likely to arouse. Or at least, the masturbator isn't going to care too much whether a string of academics reckons his source of erotic pleasure is going to get into the literary history books as long as it gets him aroused. Polsky does, however, make the point that pornography's main function, apart from that intended by the pornographer and the customer, is to help preserve society's double institutionalising of legitimate sex by providing images of sex that accommodate socially illegitimate desires. Society has to stigmatise pornography to establish what is unacceptable—in other words, it's used as a safety valve, like prostitution. Polsky's sociological look at pornography, while rather superficial in its simple attitude that pornography is primarily a masturbatory aid, is an astute summing-up of society's obsession with the subject: we're always looking for touchstones and in today's topsy-turvy world a lot of people want to know what's got society's brand of approval. People just forget they *are* society.

It is precisely this need to gain our moral equilibrium that has caused the current confusion over pornography, the need to have pornography investigated, examined and judged. The logical attitude is that you can take a word like pornography, define it fairly specifically and categorise products according to this labelling. But this wouldn't give any reassurance. It wouldn't say whether it was right or wrong and, heaven forbid, books, movies and so on might have to be judged purely on their own artistic merits. To a great extent pornography exists because of the confusion over art and non-art; it's the age (it has been ever since the Industrial Revolution and the Education Act) of popular culture, where it's difficult for anyone to determine what's good and bad.

We can, quite clearly, say that pornography is the depiction of sexual activity, that it's different from eroticism, which is something created to arouse sexual feeling, and both are different from obscenity, which is a legal term that's meant to encompass all sorts of things that society at large finds revolting. We can, but no one does because pornography is a good blanket term for something that is undesirable and it leaves the door open for all sorts of arguments not about what pornography means but about what things are pornographic and, going further, what effects these various and disparate things have on us. Pornography, as a categorisable product rather than a definable description in words or images, is the invention of society. Charles Rembar had the last word when he said 'Pornography is in the groin of the beholder'.

REAR ENTRY: They do say that our British police force, in addition to many other arduous duties, has the doubtful privilege of giving value judgements to the arts. One of the trickier assessments concerns the taboo approach to anal intercourse; one might call it a hole in the Law. Not to be confused with taking from behind, another subject now discussed with enthusiasm in men's magazines. For example:

> Surprisingly, we have never done it like that and, when one of my pen pals wrote about 'taking me on all fours in front of a blazing fire'—it was winter at the time—I didn't rest until I got Peter to do it. He was watching TV, in his pyjamas, and I sat at his feet, just at the right height and, when he was on the point of wanting to ejaculate, I raised my nighty and presented my bottom to him, on all fours. Thus, I had my first knowledge of that joy while watching the late night bulletin.
>
> *Men Only*. Vol 37, No. 3. (See also *Lady Chatterley*.)

LITTLE RED SCHOOLBOOK: is an English edition of a Danish manual for school-kids. With its red cover and pocket size, it (deliberately) recalls the *Thoughts of Chairman Mao* and the similarity was too much for us to take in England. The *LRS* was prosecuted for being obscene, anti-authoritarian and foreign. We don't want any of this Scandinavian permissiveness over here, seemed to be the magistrates' opinion and the worst crime of all was to actually give the facts to children—at least without lacing them with the usual heavy dose of morality, as if sex could only be taken like medicine.

The *LRS* wasn't (and isn't: a revised version, issued after the trial, cut out the offending 20 pages on sexual matters) a sex manual for kids, but more of a children's charter, expressing and, to be fair to its critics, exhorting independence from authority whether at home or at school. The prosecution for obscenity of its British publisher, Richard Handyside, was a farce.

The thinking in the *LRS* itself is much clearer and more logical than the thinking of either its critics or its defenders. Its 1971 trial said more about England than about children or the book itself. It was a classic British occasion. Liberals couldn't take the *LRS* either. Paul Johnson said of it in the *New Statesman*:

In our anxiety to bury Little Lord Fauntleroy we may end up with Master Shop Steward. The model child presented by the *Little Red Schoolbook* seems to me unlikely to be either attractive or happy. He (or she) gets books on education methods from the library and instructs his teachers on their professional failings. He constantly moves the furniture around in the classroom. He drags mattresses into the corridors. He puts up posters, banners, slogans and wall newspapers. He pins material about sex education on the notice boards. He complains about the state of the lavatories ('this is one thing you really must insist on'), hands in his exam papers blank, sells soft drinks in the playground, sets up his own contraceptive shop ...

All of which, like most of the liberal guff about preserving the mystery of childhood, is to miss the point that the *LRS* addresses itself to teenagers, by which time there ain't much mystery left. As for the 'model children' currently churned out by our schools, give us the Mark-2 *LRS* child every time ...

(See also *OZ Trial,* and *Underground.*)

RUGBY PLAYERS: Early on in the Longford campaign, solid Rugby chaps expressed through their association determined support in the fight against filth:

I and the Rugby world are completely in support of Lord Longford's committee and if we can help we will be only too pleased to do so. I think our Rugby songs and jokes are mild and not of a pornographic nature. They are not sick, merely a young man's reaction to a good night out. *Sir William Ramsay, President of the Rugby Football Union.*

When I was only seventeen
When I was only seventeen
I found I had a ****
And if I struggled very hard
I could get my finger in
But now that I am twenty-four
My **** has lost its charm
And I can get my finger in
And half my ****** arm.

The Harlots of Baghdad
We are three harlots of Baghdad
We **** and fornicate like mad
We don't give a rap
For a dose of the clap
Our object is to spread disease
Syphilee, gonorhee
Our object is to spread disease.

You can have it standing up or lying down
You can have it either way for half-a-crown
Up the back, up the front
Up the navel, up the **** ...
From *More Rugby Songs*, a Sphere Original.

SCANDINAVIAN SOLUTION: The much-quoted 'Scandinavian Solution' in effect means the end of censorship or, if you prefer, the legalisation of pornography. There are several ways this could be done. Some favour legalising sex books and materials, but confining their sale to certain shops in certain areas of the city – Soho as an institution. But the simplest and most sensible solution seems to be to legalise the sale of sex books and materials anywhere, but to prohibit their sale to minors and to place comparable restrictions on their display and advertising – in other words, the same kind of regulations as apply to cigarettes and alcohol. The results of such a measure have been variously forecast as a saner society and the decline and fall of the Western world; but David Gold, a leading distributor of sex literature, estimates them as follows:

> If everything were legal, Soho would collapse. You'd see prices drop amazingly overnight ... What you'd see then is for about six months after it becomes legal, sales of the hard-core material would shoot up and sales of what I handle, which is titillating material, would go down. But after six months, I think the market would return to being exactly what it is at present: most people would buy the kind of thing we stock. The hard-core material would be available in a few specialist shops for those who want it, but at lower prices. (From an interview in *Time Out*.)

SEX EDUCATION: Clearly, if one believes that sexual activity must include an emotional involvement, a merely technical programme becomes offensive: a parallel lesson in relationships becomes desirable to complement the technical lesson. The mistrust felt towards certain educationalists, notably Dr Martin Cole of the Institute for Sex Education and Research, arises mainly because this form of sex education concerns itself mainly with a simple programme of physiological, psychological and biological information upon which the learner is supposed to build his own morality. These, of course, may feel that as biologists their principal aim is to explain this aspect of sex and that the emotional, ethical, social and other aspects are better left to experts in those fields. Dr Cole and his colleague Dr Phillip Cauthery, however, are both well aware of the importance of sex as an intimate relationship between people, and their book *Fundamentals of Sex* (W. H. Allen 1971) emphasises the mutual happiness to be gained from a knowledge of sex learned in a broad context:

> To understand sex it is necessary for men to know something of women, and women of men. This book endeavours to give some explanation of both. Understanding should facilitate loving, unsecretive and complete communication between the sexes.

They split their aims into the social, psychological, biological and medical.

> The biological aim is to present sex within an evolutionary framework and to show that our desires are the product of natural forces essential for our survival not only as beings, but as happy beings producing an environment within which our young can flourish physically and mentally. The social aim is to try to eliminate the undue emphasis on sexual gratification which can so often lead individuals to establish relationships based on no more than the fact that the male possesses a penis and the female a vagina ... The medical aim is to try to prevent some of the destructive and harmful consequences that often arise from sex ... The psychological aim is to try to lessen inhibiting guilt and shame arising from sexual and emotional needs ...

These aims seem to us the perfect antidote to pornography and such responsibility and sensitivity to a subject is rare even within the present accepted school curriculum: would that history, religion or literature were scrutinised so minutely by educationalists.

Sex education has, however, become a dirty term synonymous with pornography because of the false claims of some magazines, books and movies (see *Magazines*, *Cinema*). Many among the glut of sex mags that flourished in 1971 claimed to provide 'sex education for adults', and a couple of years before certain film companies had exploited the same phrase. In both fields there are genuine attempts to educate in a general sense: the American *Sexology* magazine and the films *Helga* and *The Body,* for example; but most are simply exploitative and originally assumed the label to justify overt sexual content in the terms of the law: American pornographic magazines still have to carry a statement that they are of educational value. But for there to be valuable sex education, there must be teachers who know the subject and as yet sexology is not taught at Teachers' Training Colleges: it is easy for slick writers and fringe experts in psychology, sociology and biology to offer useless advice. Even today, when sex education is a major topic of controversy, the only real contributions have come from the Institute for Sex Education and Research; from people like the Danish Drs Hegler, whose *ABZ of Love* and *XYZ of Love*, are perfect examples of the 'common sense' attitude to sex; and also from the BBC–TV films aimed at children *and* adults. One attempt at sex education, a chapter in the *Little Red Schoolbook* (Stage I, 1971), was the subject of an obscenity charge and the publisher Richard Handyside was fined, although the magistrate admitted that the obscenity lay in the book's encouragement of the child's questioning of established values rather than in specific pornographic writing. The *Little Red Schoolbook*, whose advice was in fact quite sensible and would possibly not have been heard of if Handyside were not also the publisher of left-wing political literature, also prompted a *Little White Schoolbook* to assert the traditional values.

For over fifty years, sex education has been advocated as an essential part of the school curriculum. Until ten years ago there was no noticeable response to half a century's appeals but in the 1960s sex education was established despite the opposition, though to what extent this is anything more than biological information isn't clear.

Not unrelated is the fact that, in spite of advances in the past ten years or so, surveys indicate that among young people who commit sex offences, around 95 per cent had received no sex information from their parents.

Inter-Courses, a witty booklet which points this up, was written in 1970 by Maurine Hill and Michael Lloyd-Jones, and published by the National Secular Society. Herewith some extracts:

> More nonsense has been written on the subject of masturbation than on any other sexual phenomenon (e.g. Kenneth Walker, *The Physiology of Sex*).
>
> Unless control is exercised, the habit is likely to grow ... Self-reproach, shame and fear add their burdens, so the masturbator becomes affected with the mentality of the slave and the

lackey. He hates himself and his vice, and, fearing that his condition must be obvious to the whole world, tries to escape from his fellows.

This we would call pernicious nonsense.

... What we would say to boys on this subject is something like this: 'Self-stimulation (often called masturbation, wanking, shooting, pulling, tossing off, jerking off, etc). It is natural completely harmless, and usually very enjoyable. ...'

James Bevan, who is quite clear about the harmlessness of masturbation, nevertheless spreads the alarming idea that, if a girl does it by 'the thigh-rubbing method', 'she may find it difficult to open her legs and obtain excitement from coitus.' We would require evidence of this ...

The authors of many of these books make extraordinary errors, even of basic anatomy and physiology. Dawkins informs her readers: 'The left scrotum hangs lower than the right.' We are surprised that a doctor should not know that one scrotum per man is the usual quota.

TEACHER IS 'UTTERLY SICK'

I am utterly sick of Mr Lennon's private parts, and of the divine mission he appears to believe he has to display them to the teeming millions of the world. I'm sick of him and of all the other seedy, unwashed apostles of the new morality, whose gospel appears to be that in order to achieve salvation we must all fling off our clothes and copulate feverishly with every one in sight ... they are quite at liberty to go to hell in their own way, provided only that they don't interfere with me, or with anyone else.

But that I would say, is just what the people who have initiated these sex education programmes are trying to do. They amount to a deliberate attempt to interfere with—to change, in fact—the beliefs, standards, and practices of what I would call normal people ...

... And I am pretty sure that before very long, if these programmes are widely shown, there will be a big increase in sexual practices amongst children at the upper junior and early secondary stages. Instead of worrying about girls of fifteen, we could

well be worrying about having to abort girls of twelve and treat them for VD. What is probably worse, many—if not most—of these children will grow up with an entirely physical, entirely mechanised view of sex, which will give them small chance of ever knowing the real beauty which can, and should, exist in the right kind of relationship between a man and a woman.
Extracted from a speech by Robert Clegg, Headmaster, Burnley Primary School.

SMALL ADS: by which we mean small ads for sex, most often found in the underground Press like *Oz* or *International Times* or *Time Out*. Or at least they used to be found there. But last year's conviction of *International Times* for publishing classified ads in which homosexuals advertised for each other has severely restricted this form of contact. If the conviction wasn't bad enough, the Appeal Court upheld it in such all-embracing and viciously biased terms that today it is virtually illegal for one person to advertise for another for sexual purposes, no matter if the partners are male, female or beasts of the field. It seems to be fairly generally agreed, even among some 'opponents' of 'pornography', that this sort of advertising served a useful social purpose and was more a reflection of the pressures of life in a big city, especially for minorities like homosexuals, than it was any sudden sign of a national moral decadence. The ads haven't stopped completely, as a glance through the underground Press will convince you, but, like many of the other worthwhile features of the 'underground', they have been harassed and hampered unnecessarily by the law. Meanwhile the publishers of so-called 'contact' magazines—magazines containing nothing but sex small ads, many of which are fictitious or inaccurate—carry on laughing.
(See also *Obscene Publications Act* for a full analysis of the legal aspects of obscenity.)

ANNE SUMMERS: really ought to go with a picture. She was the very pretty girl who managed the first London sex supermarket. The business failed after two years, though other boutique-style sex-aid enterprises flourish. Miss Summers was engagingly reported by the *News of the World* (9.5.71) as first trying out all the products herself.

TELEVISION: It is generally fashionable to be worried about the effects of television on politics, the Vietnam War, children, the mentally unstable, the national crime figures and the nuclear family. But the serious argument for and against the ill effects of TV begins and ends in this country with the work of Mrs Mary Whitehouse and her National Viewers' and Listeners' Association.

This is a pity. It means that the question of whether or not the monolithic structure of TV should be open to outside participation, and even regulation, has been indissolubly associated in the public mind with the sort of moralising which borders on eccentricity.

Mary Whitehouse, ex-schoolteacher from Claverley near Wolverhampton, began her one-woman crusade against the media, and in particular the BBC, in 1963 when 'telling example[s] of the immediacy of television impact came my way'. The early stages of her campaign have become classics in her own write (she has written them out twice, in virtually identical terms, in *Clean-Up TV* and her autobiography '*Who Does She Think She is?*'): the 'Meeting Point' programme on BBC which drew a 'permissive' reaction from the girls she taught; the 'kitchen sink' plays in the 'Wednesday Play' series in autumn 1963; 'That Was The Week That Was' at its height during that same winter although axed by Christmas; the renewal of the BBC Charter without 'additional safeguards' in January 1964; her first public meeting at Birmingham Town Hall; the hostility of Hugh Carleton Greene, then Director General of the BBC, to the 'Clean-Up TV' campaign; the petition to Parliament; the formation of the National Viewers' and Listeners' Association in 1966. (Mrs Whitehouse's campaign began in her hostility to the productions of the BBC Drama Department and concern over the airing of the 'New Morality' on religious programmes.) *Up The Junction; Cathy Come Home; Till Death Do Us Part;* the BBC Sex Education series. What began as a campaign against 'disbelief, doubt and dirt' in all forms on television, soon narrowed to a campaign against 'dirt' alone, then broadened into part of the wider reaction against 'dirt', not just on television, but anywhere, even in Copenhagen (which seems a long way to go to look for it).

... that the men and women of Great Britain believe in a Christian way of life; deplore present day attempts to belittle and destroy it and in particular object to the propaganda of disbelief, doubt and dirt that the BBC pours into millions of homes through the television screen. And that crime, violence and illegitimacy and venereal disease are steadily increasing, yet the BBC employs people whose ideas and advice pander to the lowest in human nature, accompanying with this a stream of suggestive and erotic plays which present promiscuity, infidelity and drinking as normal and inevitable. *From the 'Clean-Up TV' Petition to Parliament.*

In an earlier Sunday afternoon series Pinky and Perky were constantly unkind to the point of callousness to the grown-up in their programme. No doubt children are much amused by this, but it is then not surprising if they feel it clever to act in a similar way. This kind of thing could be the origin of the cruelty some find it hard to understand of juvenile delinquents towards their elders.

After we had discussed the matter for some time the Director General asked 'What was wrong with last week's programme?' He was referring to 'TW3'. I then gave him an example ... Lance Percival was dressed up as Father Xmas and was singing a song about children. He referred to the children in the song as 'little bleeders'. I said to the Director General, 'First, as one who is engaged in the entertainment business "little horrors" would have been artistically a better phrase to have used. And secondly, many parents would not wish to have children referred to as "little bleeders" on television' ... He said, 'You know, I have children but it never occurred to me there was anything objectionable in children being referred to as "little bleeders".' Now there may be—clearly there are—people who take that view. It explains the difficulty of getting better standards on the BBC if the man at the top ... takes that attitude of mind. *Mr William Shepherd, MP, quoted in 'Clean-Up TV'.*

Plays of this kind [i.e. sexy or sadistic] can sap energy, tire with fear and feed with false values. *Mrs Whitehouse on the effect of plays on children.*

Already there are some programmes serving a very real social purpose. Week after week that popular programme 'Dixon of Dock Green' has brought us the tragic side of life but always with humour and drama and with a responsible objective in mind.

'You know, miss, my parents are divorced,' the other [child] said to me. 'I don't think they really wanted to be because Daddy came back four times to try to sort it out with Mummy. But I suppose they are both very proud people and they didn't know how to do it.' Don't you think it would be wonderful if they would put on plays which show people like us how to work through our difficulties and stay together instead of showing people who run to a cigarette or a drink or out through the door whenever there is trouble?

I wish that family had watched 'The Newcomers'. They might have had a glimpse of a way out of their troubles.

(*But the Clean-Up TV Campaign has demonstrated equal concern for anything on television which attacks authority and the Establishment.*)

January 1965 saw the first anniversary meeting of our campaign which coincided with the period of national mourning for Sir Winston Churchill. Mrs Buckland and I spoke that afternoon of how Sir Winston's passing had brought home with a sense of shock and shame just what had happened to the nation in the years since the war; how we faced as grave a danger in the fields of morals and faith as we faced on the battlefields of twenty years ago. The onslaught on the character of our nation gathered momentum daily with the manouevrings of the humanists, the unending publication of pornographic literature, the constant portrayal of violence as normal and perversion as acceptable.

And talking of Billy Graham what lay behind the screening of a photograph of him in 'The Young Adults' at the point when a teenager was suggesting that those who set up any standard only served to drive young people away?

When, as sometimes happens, I am shouted down or laughed at by students, it helps to remember that those really responsible for the present permissive trend in our society are my own generation. We have come to terms with so much. In our anxiety not to be thought square we have little established shape left at all and we have, by and large, created a candyfloss society in which the young can find little of hard substance on which to cut the teeth of conviction.

I wrote ... to protest about the screening of the 'In View'

programme on the police at the time of the Shepherd's Bush police murders [and] *For the West,* the play about the Congo . . . representing the white mercenaries of the Congo as sadistically cruel, totally self-interested and without a trace of the bravery which saved the lives of hundreds of people, black and white.

(*In fact, its concern for the preservation of authority led it into seeing anything opposed to authority as part of a subtle conspiracy—hippie or communist-inspired, or both.*)

A conspiracy? I do not know. I only know that to me there seems a remarkable unawareness both of the delicacy of minds and hearts and of the whole lesson of history: without courage, faith and hope a nation perishes. And if you batter a nation into withdrawal and cynicism, what have you left? Raw and pliant material for an alien philosophy.

In many little ways there appears to be a deliberate attempt to get children preoccupied by violence.

As time went on we became convinced that pornography was being used as a political weapon and this belief was strongly reinforced by a letter in the *Sunday Times* (9/8/70) which drew attention to a paragraph from *Cinema Documents,* a publication produced under the supervision of the Italian Communist Party.

Nov. 9th 70: Phone call from Mr John Hopkins, one of the Yippies who took part in the Frost Programme. He told me the group had met yesterday morning with a member of the Shadow Cabinet—now I wonder who that could be—and 'other prominent politicians who sympathised with our aims'. One of the outcomes of this meeting was that they should challenge me to open debate—'We know this would get a lot of publicity and it would be a very good way of getting our views across.'

I let him talk as I wanted to get as much out of him as possible—he told me he was speaking from the HQ of the Institute of Contemporary Arts—I believe this is supported by Arts Council money—played for time and asked for a telephone number where I could contact him later in the day. Bit reluctant to give it to me, but did in the end. Shortly afterwards one of the dailies rang—could I help them to 'run the Yippies to ground at all'—so I gave them the telephone number Hopkins had given me. Felt a bit funny afterwards, so was all the more pleased when the local policeman on instructions from a good deal higher up came to take charge of me. Funny thing, felt quite scared today. I suppose it's one thing to watch revolutionaries in action on a television screen, quite another to have them speak to you and to know that they know where you are!

(*Those who, like the authors, know Hoppy personally can estimate for themselves the threat he posed to Mrs Whitehouse's safety, then or at any other time.*)

I owed much to the Oxford Group and to MRA for it was through these movements that I found again my personal faith and developed that concern for the country which, along with my deep sense of responsibility for the children I taught, led me into this campaign.

So much for the effects of television on Mrs Whitehouse. What about the effects of Mrs Whitehouse on television? Certainly the 1960s are over. Mrs Whitehouse correctly identified 1963 as the 'climatic year' of 'TW3', the 'Wednesday Play', 'Honest to God' and the Profumo Affair. By 1965 Sydney Newman, then Head of BBC TV Drama, had issued two memoranda to his staff cautioning them in their treatment of sex and violence. By 1967, Harold Wilson (who had been involved in a feud with the BBC), had appointed Lord Hill from the ITA as the new BBC Chairman. On 16 July 1968, Hugh Carleton Greene, Mrs Whitehouse's arch enemy, ended his reign as the BBC's Director General.

Mrs Whitehouse was less vociferous about television after Greene left. She moved on to wider fields and pastures blue, allying with Lord Longford and Malcolm Muggeridge in their general campaign against pornography. It is too early to estimate how much she contributed to the emasculation of British television at the end of the 60s. Emasculation it most certainly was, as Kenneth Adam revealed in his 'Take Over at the BBC' series in the *Sunday Times*. Today, controversy over 'TW3' and the Wednesday Play has been replaced by controversy over *Yesterday's Men* and *Casanova*. How have the mighty risen beyond reproach!

Milton Shulman, TV critic of the *Evening Standard*, summed up television and the Whitehouse Years this way:

Fear is behind the instinctive support that Mrs Whitehouse

now gets from so many people. Parents are anxious and ignorant about the new morals and the new attitudes of a generation that finds little solace in religion, recognises the advent of the pill, flirts with the excitement of a drug culture. It is a real fear and television is partly responsible for much that is wrong with our society today. But by concentrating her attack on the sexual element of TV, Mrs Whitehouse is merely encouraging those people who would want the media to become even more timid, more orthodox, more conformist, more trivial than it already is. That is the real corrupting aspect of television.

THEATRE: Britain's official censor, the Lord Chamberlain, reigned for 231 years. He was finally abolished in 1968. Before his demise the avant-garde had long fought angrily for experiment and the American underground had danced its seven veils away. Political censorship was made to look notoriously restrictive in the light of the satire shows which burst upon the television screens from 1963, and sexual exposure had much stronger impact on the film screen.

Changing taste continues to make one era's pornography another's family entertainment, but it would now take a heated imagination to accept the notion of *Mrs Warren's Profession* as a 'dramatised stench' (one contemporary description of Bernard Shaw's play about prostitution) or fret too deeply over a flushing lavatory—offstage. Current naked bodies treading the boards, group gropes, simulated copulation and that extra blush of language may mean more to freedom than to art. There is pseudery attached to nakedness as much as hypocrisy attached to the *double entente*. But the death of the censor has not brought a rush of legal action. The penis is more in evidence than the penalty.

The following quotations make up a package and we allow *on* mark to the late Lord Chamberlain against the less engaging lunacie which emerge when the individual sits in judgment over taste. A complaint reached his office over the word 'maidenhead' used in a revue. To which he replied:

> Dear Sir, Maidenhead is a town in Berkshire, in which 17,000 people contrive to live without embarrassment.

On the other hand, no marks for bringing Edward Bond's *Save* to Court in 1965: serious violence (a baby stoned to death) in a serious play.

What is a censor of plays? He is an official of infinite wisdom, infallible judgment, and encyclopaedic erudition for whom time does not exist. That is a fiction that never came to life. *Bernard Shaw.*

I have studied Ibsen's plays pretty carefully and all the characters in Ibsen's plays appear to me morally degraded. *E. F. Smythe Pigott* (*Lord Chamberlain*).

The humiliating thing is to have to go to St James's Palace and haggle – e.g. 'bugger' disallowed, but a 'fart' or two handed back by way of consolation. Perhaps most sickening of all – a scene in which a man beats his mistress, of which the L.C.C.'s representative said 'We'll allow that if it takes place behind the furniture.' *David Mercer.*

There must be no scratching of private parts. Charles Wood, *Meals on Wheels.*

... Armstrong's *Last Goodnight*, where a sixteenth-century lowland Scot refers to a Highlander as a 'draff-black bare-arse horse-turd Hielanman'. 'Horse-turd' was cut by the censor, 'bare-arse' was allowed. Why on earth? The one referred to the man's kilt, the other to an old Scots legend that the first Gael was created by God out of a pile of horse droppings, which, although not flattering, was a correct reflection of the racial feelings of the period. *John Arden.*

Homosexuality dominated the attentions of the censor in the 1950s. Writers like Tennessee Williams and Arthur Miller (*A View From The Bridge*) suffered alongside Sartre (*Huis Clos*). For *Separate Tables,* Terence Rattigan had to change the Major's secret offence from picking up men in public lavatories to picking up ladies in the cinema. A revue sketch *On the Brighter Side* brought an anxious moment with the line 'there are fairies at the bottom of my garden'. John Osborne's *A Patriot For Me* could only get a club presentation, and this after the Chamberlain's change of attitude in 1958, hustled by the defiance of theatre management. It ran to packed houses and a financial loss of £16,500.

The Chamberlain cannot allow such scenes as a homosexual ball at which some of the men are dressed as women (including one who plays Lady Godiva dressed in a gold lamé jock-strap).

The laws of decency and order must be administered by someone, and it is better far to check before than to correct after. The preliminary stroke of the kindly blue pencil in a tentative play or sketch is better than the spreading of objectionable matter. Hundreds of ears may be poisoned before the remedy is found. *Clement Scott,* 1892.

If it comes to prohibiting, there is not aught more likely to be prohibited than truth itself whose first appearance to our eyes bleared and dimmed with prejudice and custom, is more unsightly and plausible than many errors. *John Milton.*

The script of *Pick-Up Girl* was submitted to the Lord Chamberlain ... He demanded that the words syphilis, abortion and miscarriage should be deleted from the play. There was a line of five words to which he objected. During the court proceedings the judge asked a question concerning the defendants. In reply the police constable said, 'They were both wearing nothing.' This line was considered unfit for public performance.
Peter Cotes, *No Star Nonsense*, 1949.

It is a far cry from the scandal of *Pygmalion.* According to Peter Fryer, in his history of Grundyism, 'bloody' was never used between the notorious cry of Eliza Doolittle in 1912 and Noel Coward's *Red Peppers* in 1936.
Richard Findlater, *Banned.*

The banned line in the Income Tax Song, 'He's almost definitely queer': this line must be totally eliminated and no substitute referring to the Income Tax Inspector as a homosexual will be allowed. In Act One, Scene 2: The stage directions at the commencement ... are not observed. Jack is lying on top of Deirdre instead of sitting on the bed. When he removes himself Jack's shirt is to be seen outside his trousers, and the later dialogue is punctuated by his stuffing it back. Deirdre's slip remains outside the whole time. Requirement: Jack and Deirdre must sit on the bed as allowed. They may not lie. Jack must be fully clothed, not in deshabille, and Deirdre's slip must be inside her breeches. 1959 Leeds production of *The World of Paul Slickey*. (Quoted in *Banned*, Richard Findlater.)

What matters is what the censor does not to what I have written, but to what I might have written.
Leo Tolstoy.

A magistrate has laws to administer; a censor has nothing but his own opinion. A judge leaves the question of guilt to the jury; [see *OZ Trial*] the censor is jury and judge as well as lawyer ... The law may be only the intolerance of the community, but it is a defined and limited intolerance. *Bernard Shaw*.

As if to confirm their worst fears, and almost as a ritualistic celebration of the censor's disappearance, the American musical *Hair* made its entrance virtually on the heels of the censor's departure. It contained everything in the sexual field the Lord Chamberlain was entrusted to protect us against. Not one four letter word but all of them; full frontal nudity of both sexes; heterosexual and homosexual themes; songs proclaiming the glory of free love, masturbation and marijuana. Instead of being rushed into the courts to face an obscenity charge, *Hair* in less than three years has acquired such an image of respectability that it has become an acceptable school treat for 13-year-old girls and Princess Anne could be seen dancing on the stage after seeing it without producing any serious threat to the monarchy. Milton Shulman, *Evening Standard,* May 13, 1971.

Though Moral Re-Armament still existed, it was heard from little. Early in the decade, it ventured on a spectacular and comic action in Edinburgh; at the Festival, a theatrical 'happening' had been staged, in which for a few seconds a glimpse was caught, by exceptionally wide-awake members of the audience, of a girl who might well, according to some who saw the event, have been naked. Local MRA members began an agitation and eventually brought a prosecution against the organisers for an indecent exhibition, several of them going into the witness box to declare that they had seen a naked girl and been profoundly shocked.

One of them, from his demeanour, suggested that the sight of a naked girl might well have shocked him, or even unhinged his reason entirely, but he rather weakened this Saint-Anthony-like impression by claiming to be a journalist, and, on being pressed as to the nature of his journalism, producing as the only example he could actually remember a letter he had once had printed in the *Scotsman*. Bernard Levin (re 1963) in *The Pendulum Years*.

The political aspect of censorship was always the most irksome to serious writers and directors—the RSC's *US* was almost banned altogether and many cuts were demanded. The American *Macbird* was banned, though it was performed in a club production. The RSC could not present *In the Matter of J. Robert Oppenheimer*. Rolf Hochhuth's *Soldiers*, centre of much bitter controversy, was banned for its portrayal of Churchill as Sikorski's murderer. (The idea that the theatre has an obligation to be fair is surely carrying fair play to unreasonable limits.) Gillian Hanson, *Original Skin*.

Let a collection of Yahoos only take off their clothes, cavort about the stage and yell obscenities, and a great breakthrough in dramatic art is announced and applauded. *Malcolm Muggeridge*.

In our culture an artist is expected to move the reader. He is supposed to move him to tears, to laughter, to compassion, even to hatred; but he may not move him to have an erection, or to mockery of public figures making a spectacle of themselves ... By these restrictions we doom ourselves to a passionless and conformist community. *Paul Goodman*.

Where a player is required to be naked or simulate sex acts he or she must be told in advance of audition. Before a player is required to undress he or she must be auditioned as an actor, singer or dancer. Where nakedness is required at an audition, an Equity observer must be present. Sex acts will not be required at auditions. Managements must give every aid to players in legal difficulties because of a directed performance. The meaning of a sex act is anything which if performed in public would be regarded as an 'indecent act' and the meaning of nudity is a state of undress which if seen in public would be regarded as 'indecent'. British Equity rules, as quoted in *Plays and Players* November 1969.

Our release from the bondage of the Lord Chamberlain has not plunged us into anything very lurid. The glimpse of a bare breast (*Blue Comedy*), rampant homosexuality and glimpse of a bare penis (*Fortune and Men's Eyes*), hippy hysteria and mixed nudity carefully censored by back lighting (*Hair*), two married queers having a baby (*Splitting Image*), and salty language plus cunnilingus (*The Beard*) may sound daring by previous standards, but they hardly add up to a paradise for the prurient or make much of an advance in theatrical liberty. *Felix Barker*, writing at the end of 1968.

I think it is disgusting, shameful and damaging to all things American. But if I were 22 with a great body, it would be artistic, tasteful, patriotic and a progressive religious experience. *Shelley Winters on onstage nudity.*

(See also *The Dirtiest Show in Town.*)

TRIALS: The two most memorable recent trials have been dealt with separately: *Lady Chatterley* and *Oz* Magazine. The following is a small historical round-up, 90 per cent of it in the world of books.

In 1915, D. H. Lawrence's *The Rainbow* was burned (to the tune of 1,000 copies) without any prosecution—or therefore, any chance of its adequate defence ... *Ulysses* was left alone, though its importation in single copies from France (where it was published in 1922), was being achieved through many stratagems, including that of binding it up in the covers of a *cordon bleu* cookery book.

1928. A Bow Street magistrate orders the destruction of Radclyffe Hall's novel about lesbian love *The Well of Loneliness*.

In 1929 the Postmaster-General, acting under the powers given to him by the Post Office Act of 1908, intercepted in the mails a group of D. H. Lawrence poems collected under the name of *Pansies*.

Also in 1929, Lawrence's paintings at the Warren Galleries

were raided by the police on the grounds that they showed pubic hair.

In 1932, the eccentric and self-named uncrowned King of Poland, Count Geoffrey Wladislas Vaile Potocki de Montalk was prosecuted for some translated poems of Rabelais and a parody of Verlaine. Claiming his religion as paganism, he agreed to swear by Apollo. 'Members of the Jury,' said the Recorder (himself the author of verses of monstrous banality but no obscenity) 'are you going to allow a man, just because he calls himself a poet, to deflower our English language by popularising these words?' They were *not* and Montalk served six months in Wormwood Scrubs, describing his experiences in the pamphlet *Snobbery With Violence*.

From C. H. Rolph's *Books in the Dock*:

As recently as the 1950s they [pin-up merchants] were being sent to prison. If you go round some of the prisons today you will see the walls of cells and workshops decorated with the very pin-ups they went to prison for publishing. In 1961, at Surrey Quarter Sessions, a commercial magazine publisher was sent to prison for 9 months for publishing an illustrated booklet called *Scanties*, though it could not have conceivably 'corrupted' anyone.

Rolph again:

In 1953 there had been an Interpol Conference at Oslo, and the suppression of obscene literature was on its agenda. Interpol is not, as some TV pupils suppose, an international corps of tight-lipped Bonds patrolling the world in Bentleys, hovercraft and bullet-proof pullovers, and tackling criminals too powerful and dangerous for slow-moving national police forces. It's a system of communication with a small secretariat in Paris and an aptitude for arranging conferences in surroundings of splendid scenery.

In 1953, unsurprisingly, the Conference saw a cause of crime, especially sex crime, in the reading of pornography. The British 'purge' came in 1954, and the main challenge from *The Philanderer*, published by Secker and Warburg and acquitted. Counsel for the Prosecution, none other than Mervyn Griffith-Jones (who featured porminently in the trials of *Lady Chatterley*, *Fanny Hill* and real life Stephen Ward). Is the act of sexual passion 'sheer filth'? queried the liberal judge.

1960 was the year of 'the expert witness' and 1961, the year of *The Ladies Directory*, advertising prostitutes, 10 guineas for a full, illustrated page, and 1965 the year when, in Regina v. John Calder Publications Ltd, obscenity was held to include making people want to take drugs (*Cain's Book* by Alexander Trocchi).

In 1965, Britain at last wrestled with *Fanny Hill*, first published in the eighteenth century.

> Mr Hutchinson (for the defence): 'It was put to you with horror that these girls had enjoyed sex immensely. Does that horrify you?'
>
> Peter Quenell: 'It horrifies me less than it does Mr Griffith-Jones.'

This time Mr Griffith-Jones's 'horror' won out.

Then in 1967 Sir Cyril Black MP (official of the Social Morality Council) took out a summons against a London bookseller for having copies of *Last Exit to Brooklyn*, by Hubert Selby Jnr. Bernard Levin's witty account (from *The Pendulum Years*) is too good to miss:

> The first shots in the encounter were fired by Sir Charles Taylor, the Member of Parliament for Eastbourne and one of those granite survivals from the Jurassic Age which are occasionally to be found sticking up out of the more recent deposits. How he came to read this book is one of the great mysteries of the decade, but the effect it had on him he hastened to communicate to the House of Commons with a demand that proceedings should be started at once against it. The force of his plea was somewhat diminished, however, by the fact that he refused to identify the book, and since not even the Director of Public Prosecutions could be expected, Herod-like, to prosecute all the books published in the previous six months in the hope that he would thereby catch the one that had upset Sir Charles—[it might never have reached Court if Better Books hadn't wisely picked up on publicity].

The publishers won on appeal, and the Courts no doubt regretted the loss of Mr Mervyn Griffith-Jones who had been transferred to the Bench.

Worth noting, and certainly worth reading, are parallel adventures in the States as described by leading Counsel Charles Rembar who so skilfully defended *Lady Chatterley*, *Tropic of Cancer* and *Fanny Hill* on several separate occasions. One general point from his book *The End of Obscenity* (Andre Deutsch, 1969):

A curious phenomenon in censorship is the censor's personal immunity to the infectious book. The moral fibre in jeopardy is always somebody else's. In not one of these trials did the prosecution produce a witness – or his doctor, or his clergyman – who as a result of his reading, suffered physical, moral or spiritual deterioration.

UNDERGROUND: or the Alternative Society. Loose name for a collection of young newspapers, magazines, alternative institutions and a lifestyle of which free and open sexuality is a major component. The underground has consistently pioneered the use of sex material as propaganda in this country with magazines like *Oz* and newspapers like *International Times* featuring plenty of boobs and better in their heydays. This has brought the underground under fire both from the law and more recently from within its own ranks – Women's Lib have criticised the implicit exploitation of women in underground papers. But the law remains the chief enemy. 1971/1972 alone has seen four major obscenity-type trials (five if you include the trial of Paul Ableman's compilation about oral sex – *The Mouth*. Ableman, while not strictly an underground figure, is certainly a sympathiser) directed against underground organs: the trials of *Oz*, *International Times*, the *Little Red Schoolbook* and *Nasty Tales* (pending as we go to press). In all these cases, the motive for prosecution seems to have been the underground's linking of open sexuality with the call for political and social revolution, and the 'corruption' involved as much the undermining of authority in general as of morals in particular. The underground Press has also been a pioneer in the free use of 'obscene' language in print and in opening its advertisement columns to general ads for contraceptives and sex aids and to individual small ads for sexual partners. (See *Oz Trial*, *Small Ads*, *Little Red Schoolbook*, the *Obscene Publications Act* and *Politics*.)

REPORT OF THE US PRESIDENTIAL COMMISSION: set up under Lyndon Johnson, which spent $2 million and 2 years on analysing effects of pornography and obscenity and erotica – the largest study of its kind ever attempted. Predictably, it convinced nobody and was rejected by President Nixon who has never even read it. Nixon also appointed one member of the Commission (as a replacement): Charles H. Keating, founder of the Citizens for Decent Literature Inc. His minority report, denouncing his fellow Commissioners and their work in much the same apocalyptic terms as McCarthy denounced Communism in high places in the 1950s, makes the most entertaining reading in the Commission document – it also provides a disturbing precedent for Lord Longford in this country.

The crucial section of the Commission's report is its research into the 'Effects of Explicit Sexual Materials'. They were the first and to date the only body to carry out a research programme in this area. Their two main conclusions were:

1. Exposure to erotic stimuli appears to have little or no effect on already established attitudinal commitments regarding either sexuality or sexual morality.
2. The Commission cannot conclude that exposure to erotic material is a factor in the causation of sex crimes or sex delinquency.

Critics of the Commission have gone all out to attack the second of these conclusions while keeping a discreet silence on the first.

The argument between the Commission and its critics (three of its eighteen members dissented from a 'conservative' standpoint) can be caricatured in this way. The Commission would argue that if sex-offenders read pornographic books, then it's probably because they are sex-offenders. The critics would argue that if sex-offenders read pornographic books then that is probably *why* they are sex-offenders. To support its case, the Commission produced a lot of statistical evidence to show that everybody read pornographic books and we're not all sex-offenders. To support their case, the critics produced a much smaller amount of evidence to show that delinquents in general read more porn than the rest of us; but then they went on to spoil their own argument by dropping more than one hint that they consider, well, most of us *are* sex-offenders, morally at least. And anyway who cares about science when the moral fibre of the free world and the future of civilisation itself are at stake?

But the critics were right about one thing. This was a 'runaway commission' in the technical sense of the term. Set up by Congress in 1967 to investigate 'a matter of national concern' and to 'recommend advisable, appropriate, effective and constitutional means to deal effectively with the traffic in obscenity and pornography', it ended, in 1970, by recommending the removal of legal restrictions on the sale of porn to adults, a massive programme of sex education in schools and colleges and tighter restrictions on the sale of porn to minors and on sending sexual material through the post to anyone who hadn't asked for it. This is the so-called 'Danish solution' (see *Scandinavian Solution*). Chaired by William B. Lockhart of the University of Minnesota Law School and a member of the American Civil Liberties Union, it was a liberal Commission which came up with some surprising facts:

1. Pornography is not a 'matter of national concern' to most people in the USA.

2. Pornography is not as big a business as people think, at least in its explicit forms (i.e. if you don't include the normal run of advertising and movies as 'pornographic' on the grounds that they have some or any sexual content). The Commission found that 'the mail-order erotica business is very tenuous and stories that vast fortunes have been made overnight are largely apocryphal'; that 'there are no great fortunes to be made in stag film production'; that exploitation films account for only $60 million out of a total take of $1.065 billion by the US film industry in a year (1969).

3. Women enjoy and respond to pornography/erotica as much as men.

4. The Commission abandoned any attempt to define 'pornography' and 'obscenity' as a waste of time. They say:

> Some people equate 'obscenity' with 'pornography' and apply both terms to any type of explicit sexual materials. Other persons intend differences of various degrees in their use of these terms. In the Commission's report the terms 'obscene' or 'obscenity' are used solely to refer to the legal concept of prohibited sexual materials. The term 'pornography' is not used at all in a descriptive context because it appears to have no legal significance and because it most often denotes subjective disapproval of certain materials rather than their content or effect.

5. In a fascinating sidelight on Lord Longford's Committee, the US Commission decided, on the basis of intensive analysis, that Citizens' Action Groups

> may be interpreted as an attempt to reinforce and restate systems of values and behavioural standards which are perceived to be disintegrating. Because a number of people will no longer voluntarily subscribe to these standards under the pressure of informal sanctions, an attempt is made to arouse the community to a reaffirmation of values and standards in this area and to

> formalise them with new external sanction systems, usually in the form of new laws or prosecutions under the existing laws.

In other words, groups like Longford's Committee aren't really looking at pornography. They're trying to bring down the divorce rate or stop unmarried people having it away. And using pornography as a scapegoat whose effects they assume rather than investigate.

6. Other Commission findings which have a bearing on the Longford extravaganza are that

> there is a correlation between experience with erotic materials and general attitude to sex ... persons who are more sexually tolerant are also less rejective of sexual materials.

On the other hand

> persons who are older, less educated, religiously active, less experienced with erotic materials or feel sexually guilty are most likely to judge a given erotic stimulus obscene.

A lot of the Commission's findings aren't surprising at all. Some of their work comes under the well-known definition of sociology as a discipline which exists to prove that what most people think it true at any given time is, in fact, true, by proving that most people think it at that time, and therefore it must be. Thus it comes as no great surprise to anybody that

> 80 per cent of boys and 70 per cent of girls have seen visual or read textual descriptions of sexual intercourse by the time they are eighteen

or that

> experimental and survey studies show that exposure to erotic stimulus produces sexual arousal in a substantial proportion [of subjects].

It was their attempts to prove this second point that led to most of the ridicule critics tried to pour on the Commission. These were the well-known experiments where men and women reported the degree and length of erection, genital stimulus, etc., after viewing erotic materials. Masters and Johnson have even tried to measure arousal by direct physical and chemical means in pre-Commission days, but most of the Commission's own studies were of the survey type. Other surveys found that married couples reported more lovemaking and more discussion of sex after viewing erotic materials, that men are more stimulated by photos of nude women than of nude men and vice versa, and so on.

Clive Barnes has described these studies as 'science following painfully in the wake of common sense'. But in an area where common sense and a lot of common nonsense have such a head start, it is good to see science is at least on the right road.

The Commission also went into the more general arguments about social standards and morality in some detail. One of their surveys found that 40 per cent to 60 per cent of the American public believed that

> sexual materials provide information about sex, improve the sexual relationships of married couples, produce boredom with sexual materials, lead people to commit rape, encourage innovation in marital sex techniques and lead people to lose respect for women.

These contradictory and confused views are probably typical of most popular responses on the subject, in every country. Fairly enough, the Commission concluded:

> The current flux in sexual values is related to a number of powerful influences among which are the ready availability of effective methods of contraception, changes of the role of women in our society, and the increased education and mobility of our citizens. *The availability of explicit sexual materials is, the Commission believes, not one of the important influences on sexual morality.*

They should know!

VICTORIANA: We all know that Victorian males were a repressed lot and therefore almost by definition ready to ferment their bottled fantasies whilst their wives lay back and thought of England. The fact of hidden Victorian pornography is as well known as that of Gladstone solemnly talking to prostitutes in the London streets. These same facts are well analysed in two books crammed with neat scholarship: *The Worm In the Bud* by Ronald Pearsall and *The Other Victorians* by Steven Marcus. A glimpse of what they say is enough to remind us that there's little new to express in sexuality and that the eleven-volume 4,200 page memoir *My Secret Life* is perhaps the masterpiece of Victorian underground literature.

> Hateful in day, she was loathsome to me in bed. Long I strove to do my duty, and be faithful, yet to such a pitch did my disgust at length go, that laying by her side, I had wet dreams nightly, sooner than relieve myself in her. I have frigged myself in the streets before entering my house, sooner than fuck her ...

My Secret Life.

And still on his wife:

> While I fucked her I hated her—she was my spunk-emptier. 'Get off, you've done it—and your language is most revolting.' Off I went into my bedroom for the night...
>
> More and more this fashion of wearing drawers seems to be spreading. Formerly no woman wore them, but now whether lady, servant or whore, they all wear them. I find they hinder those chance feels of bum and cunt, of which I have had so many.
>
> *ibid.*

Marcus praises this 'secret' author's honesty, explaining that on this occasion, fantasy or 'ideality' is not blurring or distorting his powers of observation; and there is none of the self-inflation and self-aggrandizement that make most sexual memoirs so distasteful and untrustworthy—for example, the autobiography of Frank Harris.

More generally, we have the penis as 'a magical instrument of infinite powers'. Marcus explains:

> The chief sexual powers represented in *The Lustful Turk* can be rather simply outlined. They have largely to do with the sexuality of domination, with that conception of male sexuality in which

the aggressive and sadistic components almost exclusively prevail.

Each of the separate stories is in this sense identical with the others. Each begins with a virgin, reluctant, proud, chaste, a young woman in whom Nature has not yet been awakened. She then undergoes a series of violent experiences, which ritually include beating, flogging, and defloration in the form of rape. By means of these sufferings, her pride is subdued, her chastity broken, and in their place Nature-responsiveness is substituted. This concept of male sexuality is what I have earlier called the historically older or more traditional form, the form of aggressive domination. It is also the form in which male sexuality is represented in the overwhelming majority of pornographic works written during the nineteenth and twentieth centuries.

Mind you, when the ladies got going ... they could also sport aristocratic names to remind us of flagellation's unfailing interest for the aristocracy—Lady Termagant Flaybum, Lady Bumtickler, the Duchess of Picklerod, Lady Maria Castigate, Madame Birchini, Lady Harriet Tickletail and the Countess of Greenbirch. Whilst early Victorian magazines laid it on thick if not fast. Ronald Pearsall quotes from *Miss Coote's Confessions*, describing the extract as unexceptional:

> She goes on counting and thrashing the poor girl over her back, ribs, loins and thighs, wealing her everywhere, as well as the posteriors. All the spectators are greatly moved, and seem to enjoy the sight of Selica's blood dripping down till her stockings are saturated and it forms little pools beneath her on the floor.

Meanwhile, for those who liked *sex in legalistic terms*:

> Before many minutes had passed the coy lady was spread upon the heath couch, and Capias was duly 'entering an appearance' in a court in which he had not practised before; but which, as there was no 'bar' to his 'pleadings', he contrived to make a very sensible impression. His few 'motions' were rewarded with a verdict of approval...

Or semen fixation plain:

> Drench her little stomach and thighs with almost a supernatural flood of sperm ... heavy pattering sounds announced the return of the fluid which fell in large drops upon the carpet, and ran in

rills down her beautiful thighs (*The Amatory Experiences of a Surgeon* 1881).

Or semen poetic—from *The Three Chums*:

Side by side on the sofa, with heads reversed, they sucked each other's parts like two bees, till the last drop of honey love had been extracted.

Or just sacrilegious verse:

See him rise, with pride ascending,
Oft in favoured sinners lain,
Thousand thousand crabs attending
Swell the triumph of his train;
Hallelujah! Hallelujah!
Rises prick to fall again.

(Quoted by Ronald Pearsall)

The frustrations of that vigorous age, steeped in Church, Empire building and an open approach to death, naturally produced a button-bursting sexual undergrowth, the pornographic imagination stretched that degree wider though the prose was often feebler than in the examples cited. The bid for sexual extremes showed a few surprises maybe: Pearsall mentions verse where the 'spooney Jews' masturbate upon Christ on the cross; *le vice anglais* is established as the whip and there is an added obsession with pre-pubescent children. Otherwise ...

Perhaps the language used was one degree more expressive than the present wave of scientific baldness, at least in such mid-Victorian words as 'Back-gammon' for sodomy, 'Ballum ranorum' for the dance of naked prostitutes and 'Pegging crib' for brothel. And where euphemism is required to express a sad, factual affair, it gives comic relief against the harsh descriptions of today's public lavatories. Strictly outside Victoria's reign (1833), a Member of Parliament, W. Bankes, was accused of 'standing behind the screen of a place for making water against Westminster Abbey walls, in company with a soldier named Flower, and of having been surprised with his breeches and braces unbuttoned at ten at night, his companion's dress being in similar disorder'.

Finally, in case one should imagine that the newly invented camera wasn't put to effect, it was, via prints stuck on books with glue, and the lantern slide. Economic problems considerably reduced the potential of pictorial pornography, though before the camera's invention there had been the lithograph. Thus in 1845, a dealer was arrested having in his possession '12,346 obscene prints, 393 books, 351 copper plates, 188 lithograph stones and 33½ hundredweights of set type'. (*The Worm in the Bud*, Ronald Pearsall, a Pelican Book, 1971).

VIOLENCE: 'The pornography of violence' has become the liberal's current escape clause. Does it really exist in pornographic terms? Brutalising effects in the cinema suggest a correlation with sex, but the two are not essentially interlinked. In proper pornography, violence is in one sense ritualised (see *Whips*) rather than becoming an undisciplined orgy of blood, though there is a branch of entertainment as a whole (not merely pornography) in which violence is the main sexual stimulant. Interested parties need look no further than *The Carpetbaggers* or that classic of female masochism *Valley of the Dolls*. In other words, if sex and violence *are* linked, it is at a deeper level than pornography and to emphasise, as British film censors have been doing in recent years, the particular need to censor movies which associate the two, surely misses the point. If there is a case for censorship, it must be to censor violence *per se* regardless of any sexual reference! Discuss.

WAR: From an article by Sefton Delmer who was in the Psychological Warfare branch of the Foreign Office in 1941 and thought up porn as propaganda. (*T.L.S.* 21.1.72):

Reaction of Sir Stafford Cripps—'If this is the sort of thing we have to do to win the war', he told Sir Anthony Eden, flourishing the offending script in his trembling hand, 'I would rather lose it!'

Another offending article was a large penis given to a photo of Hitler with the caption: 'This is a most appalling forgery. Everyone knows the Fuhrer does not possess anything of the kind.'

Gone are those jokey days however, and Mr Delmer is a bit doomy about present hard times:

> I do think that the Pornowave is a symptom of the moral deterioration of our western society just as the graffiti in the underground corridors of the Maginot Line were a symptom of the deterioration in the discipline and morale of the French army, a deterioration which led to its ultimate disintegration and defeat.

WARHOL:

> 'Art will be remembered with distaste. Westerns, pornography, science fiction, rock 'n' roll, pop art paintings are the supernatural truth, the unreal place where you really are, the place where your vision is.' *Andy Warhol.*

WHIPS: The whip, as we have mentioned elsewhere, is presented in popular mythology as an English vice, connected with British public schools and a Bognor Regis shop that sells a large quantity of canes. But it has universal application, too, notably among the Japanese. It is a central feature of pornography (read France's *The Story of O*), and when photographed in action for pornographic magazines is lacking in aesthetic merit. The psychology of beating cannot be treated lightly and we leave it out.

Two points of interest. The titles of modern flagellatory magazines are amusing in a punning sort of way, where the Victorians had a certain elaborate charm.

Victorian example—Madam Birchina's Dance, A Modern Tale, with Original Anecdotes collected in Fashionable Circles. By Lady Termagant Flaybum.
Modern titles—Arduous Figure Training at Bondhaven, Swish Bottom, Fearful Ordeal in Restraintland, Screaming Flesh, The Savage Sorority and *Battling Babes.*

Point two. It was discussed at immense length in the early correspondence of *Penthouse* magazine, frequently as a toning up process for love-making. A typical letter from *Penthouse,* Vol 2, No. 5:

> I was moved by the letter of your correspondent Mrs O.V. Vol 1, No. 11) especially as her case closely parallels my own. During our engagement, I played a series of rather childish jokes on my husband, until in sheer exasperation, he turned me over, bared my bottom and spanked me—not very severely. Talking it over afterwards, we both rather shame-facedly admitted to having enjoyed it. My only complaint—and it was sincere though I am at a loss to say why—was that he had not given me a chance to take my own pants down. He laughingly promised that he would do so in future, and spankings now form a not-infrequent part of our sex life.

XENOPHOBIA: (a morbid dislike of foreigners)

On September 17, 1970, a fur farmer in upper New York wrote me regarding migrant Puerto Rican and American workers whom he has employed over the last twenty years. The gentleman advised: 'There has been a big change in our workers in the last year or two.' He stated that they have changed from rather manly, decent people to rapists being obsessed with sex, including many deviations. 'I believe,' he said, 'this is mostly due to obscene literature and obscene pictures such as I am sending you.' Charles H. Keating, dissenting commissioner on the American *Report of the Commission on Obscenity and Pornography*.

YONI: This is just to remind us of a certain poetry in sexual language, mostly missing from today's hardy manuals and more easily reflected in Eastern writing which in turn had an effect on the much-vaunted Indian love temples. This is not to suppose that public behaviour is as free as in the West. It isn't. Nevertheless, Vatsayana's immortal *Kama Sutra*, written between the third and fourth centuries A.D., is recommended reading as much for its tenderness and lyricism as for its sixty-four positions of love making. Fawn Brodie, in her biography of the Victorian explorer and translator Sir Richard Burton, writes:

> In translating the most explicit libidinal matters, Burton and Arbuthnot adroitly managed to escape the smell of obscenity. Their words were cool and delicate; they used the Hindu terms for the sexual organs, 'yoni' and 'lingam', throughout.

When, in 1962, the book was formally published in England and the United States, reviewers expressed almost unanimous surprise that it should for so many generations have been counted pornographic. The public should be grateful, Francis Watson wrote ironically,

> that after whole forests have been felled to publicise a modern rediscovery of the female orgasm, we could have the matter settled in a classical dissertation of six pages.

ZOÖPHILIA, ZOÖRASTY:
see *Bestiality*.

THE PILGRIM'S PROGRESS
A GAME IN WHICH THE PILGRIM ATTEMPTS TO STOCKPILE CREDITS IN HEAVEN WHILE TRAVELING FROM THIS WORLD TO THAT WHICH IS TO COME!
THE PATH OF RIGHTEOUSNESS
NO SCORE PATH FOR ORDINARY FOLK WITH A JOB TO DO
THE HILL OF PRIGISH-NESS
HE FINDS A GLADSTONE BAG
THE PILGRIM
THE VALE OF SELF DECEPT-ION
HE MEETS PROSTIT-UTION
THE PRISON VISITING
THE BLACK HOLE OF OH CALCUTTA
HE MEETS PORNO-GRAPHY
LECHERY AND DEBAUCH -ERY
VANITY FAIR
HE MEETS MR REASON WHY
THE FESTIVAL OF LIGHT
THE LAST DAY
THE CELESTIAL CITY
DELIVERED UNDER THE SIMILITUDE OF A COMIC STRIP---

F MOUNTS THE HILL
PRIGISHNESS----
WHAT A NICE VIEW!
---AND LET'S SEE--- I SCORE 50 POINTS.!!
---AND FINDS A GLADSTONE BAG----
OH DEAR! SWEAT --- SHE MIGHT SEDUCE SOMEONE!
BEING SEDUCED MEANS A LOSS OF 30 POINTS!
N'T
'ARD
ATE!
NOT BEING SEDUCED MEANS A GAIN OF 300 POINTS!
EACHING ---SCORE 50---
VALE OF SELF
CEPTION----
I'LL JUST DASH OFF A BOOK ON HUMILITY!
HE SCORES AN EXTRA 1000.!!
BEING HUMBLE IS SOMETHING ONE REALLY OUGHT TO SHOUT ABOUT!

HE MEETS AND ADMONISHES PROSTITUTION---
MY LIFE SLOGAN HAS BEEN TO HATE THE SIN --- BUT LOVE THE SINNER!
NOT UNLES YOU PAYS YOUR MONEY LIKE UVVER PEOPLE!
OW!
AT THE PRISON VISITING HE DISCOVERS THE GRACE OF GOD---
YES! --- THERE BUT FOR THE GRACE OF GOD GO I!
THE GRACE OF GOD IS A VERY NICE THING TO HAVE!!
GRACE OF GOD
STILL PROTECTED BY THE GRACE OF GOD---
---HE GOES OUT OF HIS WAY TO REACH THE BLACK HOLE OF OH CALCUTTA---
F*CK!
C*NT

COMPILES A
COLLECTION
PORNOGRAPHY
STUDY
I PERUSE THIS FILTH IN ORDER TO CONDEMN IT!
WHY DIDN'T WE THINK OF THAT?
SMUT
INCORPORATING 'TIT' & 'BUM'
MEETS AND ADMONISHES
AND DEBAUCHERY
THE SINS---BUT
THE SINNERS---
KINKY DEVIL!
SCORING 150
VANITY FAIR HE
A HIGHER SCORE
ANYONE ELSE
GAME---
---AND MEETS MR. REASON WHY---
THE REASON WHY I'M HERE IS I'M AT THE AGE WHEN YOU TAKE OUT FIRE INSURANCE!
PORN COMMISSION REPORT! GET YOUR PORN COMMISSION REPORT!

THEY COMPARE SCORES---
I'VE GOT 6,750 POINTS!
YES! BUT YOU'LL HAVE TO ALLOW FOR MY BEING A LATE STARTER!
AND ARE TEMPORARILY BLINDED BY THE FESTIVAL OF LIGHT---
NO SCO
THEY COMPARE SCORES FOR THE LAST TIME---
A PLACE IN HEAVEN MUST NOT ONLY BE EARNED!
SCORES
SCORES
BUT MUST BE SEEN TO BE EARNED!
CELESTIAL C
GET IN LANE
THE LAST DAY!---
GOD WILL SEE YOU NOW!
I'M SURE HE WON'T MIND MY HAVING MORE POINTS THAN ANYONE ELSE!
RIGHTEOUS PEOPLES ENTRANCE
GOD WI
SEE YOU
MR.ORDIN
FOLK!
ORDINARY FOLKS ENTRANCE

HE IS USHERED INTO THE PRESENCE OF THE ALMIGHTY!---
NO!!! NO!!!
IT CAN'T BE!!
HELLO FRANK! ---I'M GOD!
IT'S NICE TO SEE YOU!
HALLELUJAH!
AGGGHHHHHH!!!
MR ORDINARY-FOLK ALSO MEETS GOD---
GULP
I D-D-DON'T HAVE A S-SCORE GOD!
BUT MR. ORDINARY-FOLK! --- NOBODY NEEDS ONE!
YOUR FACE GOES HERE
THE END!

Other Panthers For Your Enjoyment

Man and Woman

☐ **Gore Vidal** **MYRA BRECKINRIDGE** **40p**

The elegantly outrageous novel that demolishes lots of American sexual myths. Vidal's piercing invention is at its most dazzling in this story of Hollywood sex-changes.

☐ **Martin Seymour-Smith** **FALLEN WOMEN** **40p**

The strumpet in literature – from the Old Testament right up to today's highly professional porn. The author does it with insight, sympathy and wit, and his conclusions are controversial – or, as the *New Statesman* puts it, 'Provocative'.

☐ **Trans. Charles Plumb** **THE SATIRES OF JUVENAL** **42p**

The vices – and what vices! – of Imperial Rome by one who was there. A translation for the 1970's – direct, witty, lewd.

☐ **Jean Genet** **QUERELLE OF BREST** **60p**

The criminal-homosexual world so sensuously evoked by Genet is a taboo subject in suburbia. Elsewhere, Genet is 'Matchless . . . any comment at once becomes presumptuous' – Terry Southern

☐ **Jean Genet** **OUR LADY OF THE FLOWERS** **40p**

The great sensual novel about the criminal-homosexual world with which Genet overturned middle class values.

☐ **John Rechy** **CITY OF NIGHT** **40p**

Rechy's city of dreadful night is any downtown American city after dark, when lonely homosexuals begin their frantic prowl in search of companionship.

Outsize Heroes

☐ **Henri Charrière** **PAPILLON** **50p**
Charrière, known as Papillon (Butterfly), is probably the greatest escaper of modern times not only because of his numerous indefatigable and finally successful attempts but also because of the prison he escaped from – Devil's Island. Reads like a Hammond Innes novel, yet it's stark fact, every incident verifiable.

☐ **Phillip Knightley and Colin Simpson** **THE SECRET LIVES OF LAWRENCE OF ARABIA** **40p**
Boy Scout hero or masochist. The authors examine the myth in the light of the latest information. T. E. Lawrence may well be diminished in this cool study, but he does emerge, for the first time in the numerous accounts of his ambiguous life, as a human being. 'Explosive – biographical dynamite' – *Evening Standard*

☐ **Jan Cremer** **I, JAN CREMER** **50p**
This roaring, raucous, autobiographical novel of its young author's sexual conquests in Europe and the US is scandalous, sadistic and funny.

☐ **Jan Cremer** **JAN CREMER 2** **50p**
Continues the roaring, raucous account of Cremer's one-man assault on our sacred cows – the opening moves in which were revealed to a disbelieving world in his international bestseller I, JAN CREMER. 'I'm nervous, schizophrenic, sadistic, perverted, and an inspirer of riots', Mr. Cremer admits – and lives up to every word of it.

☐ **Heinz Werner Schmidt** **WITH ROMMEL IN THE DESERT** **25p**
By a high-ranking officer of the Afrika Korps – the inside story of Rommel's vicious fight to destroy the Allies in North Africa.

☐ **William Rodgers** **THINK: a biography of the Watsons and IBM** **50p**
International Business Machines is the largest single corporation in the western world, and its policy decisions may well shape your future. Consider this: £1,000 invested in IBM when Watson started it in 1914 would be worth £6,000,000 today. This ominous account has delved into every source – except one. IBM flatly refused to give the author any information whatsoever. The reader will understand why.